Developing the experience of music ○ *Listening charts*

Developing the experience of music · Listening charts

BENNETT REIMER · *Case Western Reserve University*

EDWARD G. EVANS, JR. · *Eastman School of Music of the University of Rochester*

PRENTICE-HALL, INC., *Englewood Cliffs, New Jersey*

©1973 by Prentice-Hall, Inc., Englewood Cliffs, New Jersey

Printed in the United States of America

ISBN   0-13-294876-1
LIBRARY OF CONGRESS CATALOG CARD NUMBER   72-6253

10   9   8   7   6   5   4   3   2

Prentice-Hall International, Inc., *London*
Prentice-Hall of Australia, Pty. Ltd., *Sydney*
Prentice-Hall of Canada, Ltd., *Toronto*
Prentice-Hall of India Private Ltd., *New Delhi*
Prentice-Hall of Japan, Inc., *Tokyo*

CONTENTS

Preface   *vii*

Part 1 ○ **Concentration charts**   *1*

Rhythm (Chapter 4*)   *3*

Melody (Chapter 5)   *8*

Harmony and counterpoint (Chapter 6)   *13*

Tone color (Chapter 7)   *22*

Form · Fugue (Chapter 8)   *26*

Form · Theme and variations (Chapter 8)   *27*

Form · Fugue (Chapter 8)   *29*

Form · Continuous variations (Chapter 8)   *30*

Form · Romantic concerto (Chapter 8)   *31*

Form · Sonata-allegro (Chapter 8)   *32*

Form · Minuet (Chapter 8)   *34*

Form · Sonata-allegro (Chapter 8)   *35*

Style · Middle Ages (Chapter 9)   *36*

Style · Renaissance (Chapter 9)   *46*

Style · Baroque (Chapter 10)   *57*

Style · Classic (Chapter 11)   *69*

Style · Nineteenth century (Chapter 12)   *79*

Style · Twentieth century (Chapter 13)   *88*

*Chapter numbers are those of the textbook, *The Experience of Music,* where the topics are principally discussed.

Part 2 ○ *Perception charts*   111

Rhythm (Chapter 4)   *113*

Melody (Chapter 5)   *122*

Harmony and counterpoint (Chapter 6)   *129*

Tone color (Chapter 7)   *137*

Form (Chapter 8)   *146*

Style (Chapters 9 to 13)   *158*

Contents

PREFACE

To experience music fully, the listener must discern what is occurring from moment to moment so that his involvement is intense over the entire course of a piece. *Developing the Experience of Music: Listening Charts* has been designed to provide a simple yet effective way to help you perceive what the music is doing *as it is doing it.*

The two types of Listening Chart, Concentration and Perception, are described in the following sections of this Preface.

Concentration charts (Part 1)

By pointing out the important musical events as they take place, the Concentration Charts help you perceive and respond; they are designed as follows:

TITLE INFORMATION

After the composer's name and the title of the piece, record information is given to help you locate the selection easily in the accompanying record set, *Library for Developing the Experience of Music.*

MUSICAL ELEMENTS

At the foot of each page of every chart is an indication of the particular musical element on which the chart focuses: *Rhythm*, for example, means that the major emphasis of that chart is on the rhythm of the music, although other elements might be mentioned (it is often impossible to isolate an element completely).

In the style Concentration Charts, as in the corresponding chapters in the textbook, all the previously studied elements — rhythm, melody, harmony and counterpoint, tone color, and form — are pulled together so that the music is heard for the interrelations of the elements. These charts are intended to demonstrate the range of musical expressiveness in each style.

MEASURE COLUMN

The first column lists the measure in the musical score at which the described section of the music begins. You may ignore this column if you like, but it can prove helpful in two ways:

First, the numbers give a rough indication of the time span for each section so that you can anticipate when the next section will begin. If the first three measure numbers are 1, 35, and 40, it is clear that the section between measures 1 and 35 will take a fair amount of time while the section from 35 to 40 will go by quickly.

Second, you may wish to go further than the Listening Charts and study selected musical scores. The charts will provide a guide to your score study, helping you to locate the important musical events as they occur at each section.

For some pieces (jazz, pop, some electronic music) it is impractical or impossible to list measure numbers. Instead, only the time elapsed from the beginning of the piece is indicated in minutes and seconds (3.32 means 3 minutes 32 seconds).

CALL-NUMBER COLUMN

On one of the two stereophonic channels of the recordings you will hear a voice reciting consecutive numbers to help you keep your place as the music goes along. When a number is called, your attention is drawn to events occurring from that point to the next call number.

As you get used to the number-calling, you will find that the voice fades into the background of your consciousness, becoming not so much heard as sensed. At the same time the numbers will provide security as to the exact location in the music you have reached. (See the comments below in Strategies for Using the Concentration Charts for various ways to make use of the call-number channel.)

DESCRIPTION

The body of a Concentration Chart describes important musical happenings that you should perceive. The terms used to point out what is occurring in the music are precisely those used in your text, *The Experience of Music*, so that the charts provide reinforcement, review, and extension of textbook learnings. Elements you have focused on in the text Listenings are now heard in the context of an ongoing musical experience.

As you become practiced at following the descriptions, your eye will become more skillful in helping your ear. At first you may not be able to notice all the things going on in a particular section. As you listen to a piece again and as you use the charts more, you will discover that more of the description is noticed by your eye and more of the actual music is perceived by your ear. Soon you will become almost unconscious of the numbers' being called or the words' being read and will become highly conscious of the musical sounds and what they are doing. And the more you perceive in the music, the more involved you can become with it.

The order of items in each description generally follows the order of events in that section so that the first things mentioned are the first things heard and the last things mentioned occur just before that section is over. Terms that describe the entire section (fast, steady beat, major, high register, for example) are listed in a general order of obvious to subtle, as suggested by the music itself.

STRATEGIES FOR USING THE CONCENTRATION CHARTS

The charts may be used as (1) introduction to a chapter of the text, raising aspects to be studied, (2) accompaniment to the study of a chapter, reinforcing what is being learned, and (3) summary and review of a chapter, bringing the content together in an overview. Many charts will be used in all three ways.

As we have implied, most charts are designed to be used several times, the descriptions often being too complex to be assimilated fully in a single hearing. Rehearings are important, both for improving perception and heightening enjoyment.

With monophonic equipment the call numbers and music will be heard together, allowing the charts to be followed easily. With stereophonic equipment adjusted to balance the two channels the sound will be much like that produced by monophonic equipment. You will hear the numbers and music together, following the charts in the regular way. But you may additionally turn the channel selector to the music channel and suppress the number-calling. Now you can follow a chart with no obvious call numbers to indicate where you are. Your own perception, guided largely by the descriptions, can keep you abreast of the proceeding music. This provides an extra challenge for your ear and allows you to exercise more musical independence. So you might try listening first with the numbers loud, tuning them down as you become familiar with the music; or you might first listen with suppressed numbers, adding them later to check whether you were able to follow the chart correctly. Experiment with different approaches to feel out which seem to work best for you.

No matter how you use the numbers and charts, *be sure to listen to all pieces with no chart at all*. Although the charts will help you with many things you might otherwise have missed, they are only a means to improving your own ability to listen perceptively. So after you have studied a piece with the numbers and/or chart, put the chart away and listen on your own. Do not try to remember all the words in the description. Focus on the sounds themselves. You should find that you are able to become more absorbed in the music, with no word descriptions involved but with a keen notion of what the sounds are doing.

To help you make the transition from chart-aided to unaided listening, six records of music (from the ten records corresponding to the Concentration Charts) are available in *Listening for the Experience of Music*, a set of seven records (the seventh record contains the ethnomusic examples from the textbook's Chapter 14, Music of Other Cultures). These records contain music alone in stereophonic presentation (no voice overdubbing) so that you can enjoy the pieces at your convenience without using charts or follow charts occasionally without number-calling.

Perception charts (Part 2)

The Perception Charts give you an opportunity to exercise your musical judgment by choosing the correct description of the music out of several. Rather than offering a description of the music, as do the Concentration

Charts, the Perception Charts have you respond overtly to what you are hearing; you can thus check the accuracy of your musical perceptions.

Many of the Perception Charts have measure and call-number columns, like those of the Concentration Charts. At each call number *you are to underline the proper description from a choice of two or three*. Usually you must underline several descriptions, deciding, for example, whether the music at that point is fast or slow, loud or soft, *legato* or *staccato* or both. Your perception, in this example, must guide you to three sets of decisions.

Most Perception Charts will require several listenings in order for you to be satisfied that you have done as well as you can. The first time, underline the items you are able to perceive quickly. Each succeeding time, add to your choices and check previous choices. (Answers will be provided by your instructor.)

The Perception Charts may be used as tests, but they are conceived essentially as another means to help you perceive musical qualities and events. (The object is not just to get the right answers but to focus attention on the elements of music to become more skilled in discerning them.) Making conscious decisions about what you hear is an excellent way to sharpen your musical perception. It is also an excellent way to find out which elements are not well understood so that they may be reviewed. If you are confused about an answer, raise questions about it for clarification. Some items cannot be answered with complete objectivity. Much of music is relative, not lending itself to absolute description. Most items in the Perception Charts are quite clear-cut, with little room for debate. But some items will raise problems about the correct answer. It may well be that the suggested answer is only a bit more convincing than another or that it is impossible to choose one as being more correct than another. Where there is no clear choice, your instructor has what we believe to be the most plausible answers. If there is disagreement, use it as an opportunity to become more sensitive to the subtle shadings of musical expressiveness. Do not argue about "right" or "wrong." If an item raises a question requiring honest debate, it will have served as an excellent means to sharpening perception. So ambiguous items have been consciously included, for they are often the best items for promoting musical learning.

The Listening Charts require a very high level of concentration, making it virtually impossible to daydream while using them. Such concentration should take place with or without charts. Music deserves your undivided attention. As you improve in the ability to be absorbed in music, you will be repayed generously in heightened enjoyment.

The authors are indebted to Vincent Lawrence for his patient, expert assistance with the myriad details relating to the creation of the Listening Charts, and some preliminary work was carried out with the able assistance of Donald Metz and James Standifer.

Part 1 ∘ *Concentration charts*

Measure	Call	
1	1	Strong first-beat accents; *legato* theme begins in triple meter; *staccato* accompaniment; regular beat; simple pattern.
23	2	Strong, shifting accents.
37	3	Pace quickens; long notes against short notes; accents.
45	4	Strong emphasis on second beat; *legato* against bass *staccato*; regular beat.
57	5	Simple pattern with *legato* notes changing to *staccato* in accompaniment.
65	6	More motion; *staccato* melody; strong regular accents in accompaniment, changing from *staccato* to *legato*; ends *staccato.*
83	7	Less active pace; simple pattern (repeated notes); *legato*; some *rubato*.
95	8	*Legato* melody; *staccato* accompaniment; pace becomes more active to strong beat.
109	9	Strong emphasis on second beat: 1–*2*–3–1–*2*–3.
124	10	First-beat rest; strong *staccato* chords on beats 2 and 3.
128	11	Strong, repeated *staccato* chords in heavy accents.
132	12	Regular pulse; *legato* melody; changing to *staccato* in accompaniment; pace quickens.
144	13	Strong, regular accents; short notes.
148	14	Less active pace; *legato*; pulse weakening.

Measure	Call	
1	1	$\frac{6}{8}$ meter; fast; *staccato*; strong beat; strong accents on offbeats.
21	2	$\frac{6}{8}$ pattern continues; short, fast notes; irregular accents; very active.
37	3	Regular beat; strong accents; several simple and complex patterns.
65	4	Chords drive toward last beat of measure; alternating offbeat patterns.
88	5	Many weak accents; short-note pattern repeats in bass and brasses.
107	6	Long, accented notes in melody; short-note pattern in accompaniment.
124	7	Pattern imitated as instruments enter; becomes more active.
155	8	Syncopation, then returns to downbeats; pattern like call 1 returns.
174	9	Regular beats; long notes in melody with strong downbeat accents against short, fast notes of 1.
200	10	Repeated pattern; heavy accents.
204	11	New pattern in strings (wood of bow used); all *staccato*; strong beat.
220	12	Triplet pattern repeated; leading to heavy downbeat accents.
240	13	Repeated pattern; heavy accents; like 10.
245	14	Longer notes; heavy accents.
255	15	Very active; many accents; regular, strong beat; triplets drive toward final long note.

Measure	Call	
1	1	Triple meter; moderate tempo; emphasis on third beat shifting to first beat; simple patterns.
23	2	Return to original pattern, as at call 1.
33	3	Duple meter; more active pace; accent on last beat: ♫♩♩ ; pattern repeated several times.
51	4	New pattern: ♫♩♩♫♩ ; accents on both beats of measure.
63	5	*Staccato*; regular pulse; patterns from 2 and 3 used.
83	6	*Staccato* continues; accent on last beat; pattern constantly repeated; anticipation of return at 7.
107	7	Returns to rhythm as at beginning; third-beat emphasis; *legato*.
114	8	Simple pattern of ♩♩ ♩♩♩ ; *ritardando* to pause.
126	9	More active pace; triple meter; *staccato*; ♪♩│♪♩ pattern becomes prominent.
156	10	*Staccato* continues; ♩♩♩ pattern; ♪♩│♪♩ added.
188	11	*Staccato* continues; transition back to rhythm as at 1; *legato* to *ritardando*.
194	12	Rhythm as at beginning; emphasis shifts from third beat to first or second beat; less active pace; simple patterns.
219	13	Moderate tempo; *legato* against bass *staccato*.
233	14	Triple meter continues; more *legato*; held notes stop the motion before final cadence.

Measure	*Call*	
1	1	Slow; simple patterns; static; weight becomes heavy on second beat ("lau-*da*-te"); then all beats become weak.
12	2	Bass patterns returns ("lau-*da*-te"); *legato* accompaniment; beat becomes more steady; cadence.
24	3	More active pace; irregular accents; patterns repeated; combination of *legato* and *staccato*; strong beat.
40	4	Accented triplet pattern; *accelerando*; sudden irregular accents; strongly accented chords; *ff*; triplet pattern returns.
53	5	Voice *legato*; *staccato* chords; patterns less complex.
60	6	Patterns become more complex; vocal line contains weak accents.
65	7	Marchlike in sharp *staccato* against *legato*; simple pattern.
72	8	Patterns more simple; *legato* and *staccato* combined; note grouping shifts from duple to triple while beat remains regular.
87	9	Marchlike; strong, regular beat; *staccato* in orchestra against *legato* of voices.
99	10	Suddenly slow; like call 1; static; *rubato*.
104	11	Sudden active pace; strong, irregular accents; one shift to triple meter ("Do-mi-num").
109	12	Marchlike; *staccato*; meter shifts; irregular accents.
114	13	Pattern like 8; combination of *legato* and *staccato*; marchlike; irregular accents.
126	14	Pattern continues in voices; triplet figure in accompaniment; irregular accents; more complex.
134	15	Orchestral interlude; triplet pattern predominant; irregular accents; complex rhythms.
144	16	Strong accented chords stop the motion; like 4; *ff*.
147	17	Action pauses in preparation for final section of movement.

Measure	Call	
1	1	Long notes against short notes; irregular accents.
10	2	*Legato* with *staccato*; duple meter; strong, regular accents; pace quickening.
11	3	Regular beat with syncopation; strong accents.
25	4	Strong accents; regular beat in complex patterns.
36	5	Regular beat; repeated patterns; irregular accents.
43	6	Accented *ostinato* pattern; *staccato*; syncopation in melody.
75	7	Accented marchlike *staccato* under *legato* melody; simple patterns; syncopation.
81	8	Offbeat accents.
85	9	Accented marchlike *staccato* under *legato*.
89	10	Regular beat with syncopation; strong accents.
96	11	Strong accents under long notes.
101	12	Regular pulse with syncopation and strong accents over sustained bass.
105	13	Strong, irregular accents; irregular-beat feeling; *accelerando*.
113	14	*Legato* melody; more static; regular beat; simple pattern.
127	15	Regular beat continues; syncopation in melody.
147	16	Beat becomes stronger; *legato* melody.
161	17	Long notes in *legato*; more static; simple pattern.
169	18	Long notes in accents.
173	19	Long notes in accents over marchlike *staccato*.
177	20	Regular beat with syncopation and strong accents; long notes accented.
185	21	Strong accents under sustained note.
189	22	Syncopated pattern over sustained note.
193	23	Strong, irregular accents; irregular-beat feeling; movement quickening to cadence.

Rhythm

JOHANN SEBASTIAN BACH   Cantata 80, *Ein feste Burg ist unser Gott* (*A Mighty*
Fortress Is Our God), IV

Measure	*Call*	
1	1	Cello states *principal melodic idea*; stepwise downward, ending upward; wide range; minor.
3	2	*Principal melodic idea* in voice; cello imitates; stepwise downward, ending upward; wide range.
5	3	Repetition of idea.
6	4	Leads into long, extended line on single syllable; mostly small steps with a few leaps; wide range; cello continues *principal melodic idea* after voice cadences.
13	5	Voice has short downward pattern ending with a leap upward.
14	6	Pattern repeated a step lower.
15	7	Pattern extended into long line on single syllable; mostly small steps with a few leaps; wide range; again cello continues after voice ends.
20	8	Phrase starts smooth then becomes jagged; ends in high register.
23	9	Wide leaps; jagged; cadence.
26	10	*Principal idea* in voice again; cello imitates; stepwise downward, ending upward.
28	11	Repetition of idea.
29	12	Leads into long, extended line on single syllable; mostly steps with a few leaps; wide range; voice cadences; cello continues to end.

Measure	Call	
1	1	Orchestra states *principal melodic idea*, then shifts to decorative figure in repetitive, short pattern; quick changes in register; cadence prepares entrance of voice.
12	2	*Principal melodic idea*; major; short-phrase structure; smooth shape; orchestra imitates voice.
16	3	Second part of *principal melodic idea*; orchestra answers with decorative figure.
20	4	Repetition of *principal melodic idea*; orchestra imitates voice.
24	5	*Principal melodic idea* continues; phrase ends with long note with decoration in orchestra.
29	6	Long, stepwise melody; spins out; mostly upward; orchestra follows with decorative pattern.
40	7	Shorter phrase, much like call 1; more embellished.
43	8	Longer phrase; upward leaps; jagged; orchestra continues decoration.
49	9	Short, downward phrase; smooth; immediately repeated.
53	10	Wide leaps in melody; lower register; starts jagged and ends in smooth scalewise steps.
60	11	Short upward leaps; then long repeated notes; strong cadence; orchestra follows with decoration and strong cadence.
71	12	Repetition of *principal melodic idea*; like 1; orchestra imitates voice.
75	13	Short simple phrase; orchestra decorates.
79	14	Short-step pattern; simple pattern; immediately imitated in orchestra.
84	15	Long, stepwise melody; spins out; smooth; cadence.
89	16	Stepwise downward motion; smooth.
92	17	Stepwise upward motion; strong cadence.
98	18	Short-step pattern; like 14; imitated in orchestra; downward stepwise motion to long note over which orchestra decorates; section ends with strong cadence.

Melody

Measure	Call	
1	1	Major; mostly step motion; smooth; simple; symmetrical structure.
5	2	Smoothly downward in steps and upward in leaps; repeated.
9	3	Small steps with downward leap to long note; strong cadence.
13	4	Smooth; stepwise; short motive repeated; mostly narrow range.
18	5	Smoothly upward and downward.
20	6	Smooth; stepwise motion; cadence.
22	7	Sudden shift to minor.
24	8	Repetition of phrase from call 5.
26	9	Smooth; stepwise motion; deceptive cadences lead to strong cadence.
33	10	High register; simple, short phrases; strong but delicate cadence.

Melody

Measure	Call	
1	1	Chordal introduction; stepwise motion; narrow range.
8	2	*Main melody*; long, smooth in curved arcs of motion; small steps with large downward leaps toward end; major; wide pitch range; clarinet enters to embellish *main melody* in horn.
24	3	Large and small leaps; higher register; upward movement.
28	4	Short phrase imitated; downward.
30	5	Now upward; motion leads to call 6.
32	6	*Main melody* now in cello; many embellishments in other instruments.
39	7	Many repeated notes in nonmelodic contrast to preceding material; transition to 8.
45	8	Melodic development of material from 3; long; smooth; upward motion at end in small steps with repeated notes to 9.
56	9	Climax; tapers off in downward motion.
61	10	Small steps; downward motion continues to end the section.

Measure	Call	
1	1	Upward motion; skips then steps; major; jagged; wide range; high.
15	2	Sudden downward shift to strong cadence.
20	3	Alternating nonmelodic material and trumpet improvisatory material; clarinet "doodle" answers trumpet.
38	4	Short phrases with much syncopation; mostly stepwise; patterns repeated.
61	5	*Staccato*; short phrases repeated; strong cadences.
73	6	Higher register; smooth, short, repeated phrases in small steps.
97	7	Transition; repeated notes.
103	8	High register; wide range; syncopation; jagged; theme heard in several different instruments.
124	9	Syncopation; jagged; wide range; nonmelodic; dissonant background.
134	10	Upward; wide range; high; jagged theme in several instruments; syncopated.
145	11	Short, interrupted phrases; upward by leap.
156	12	Middle register; narrow range; repeated notes; some dissonance.
167	13	Jagged; nonmelodic; dissonant background.
173	14	Like call 1; upward; high register; jagged; wide range; high; strong cadence ends section.

Melody   *12*

SHORT SELECTIONS

EARLY ORGANUM   "Rex coeli, Domine"   Side 3, band 1

Polyphonic; nonimitative; note-against-note style; expands from unison to interval of a fourth then returns to unison; slight pause at end of phrase provides cadence feeling.

GIOVANNI PIERLUIGI DA PALESTRINA   *Missa Papae Marcelli*, I: Kyrie   Side 3, band 2

Polyphonic; imitative; six-part unaccompanied chorus; static; overlapping entrances (**stretto**).

ANDREA GABRIELI   "Ricercar del duodecimo tuono"   Side 3, band 3

Short, narrow motive treated in imitative polyphony; density expands quickly to four parts; much overlapping; strong cadence at end of section.

JOHANN SEBASTIAN BACH   Cantata 80, *Ein feste Burg ist unser Gott* (*A Mighty*   Side 3, band 4
Fortress Is Our God), VIII

Blending voices in chorale (hymnlike) style; each line a separate melody with each note forming a progression of chords; contrasting colors between orchestra and chorus; thick.

WOLFGANG AMADEUS MOZART   Requiem in d, K. 626, X: Sanctus   Side 3, band 5

Measure	Call	
1	1	*Adagio*; homophonic; melody and orchestral accompaniment with harmonic figures; thick.
11	2	*Allegro*; imitative polyphony; blending colors; thick; generally ascending.

IGOR STRAVINSKY   *Le Sacre du printemps (The Rite of Spring)*, I   Side 3, band 6

Polyphonic; nonimitative; bassoon solo; high range; additional material in contrasting woodwinds; static; thin.

IGOR STRAVINSKY   *Histoire du soldat (The Soldier's Tale)*, I   Side 3, band 7

Measure	Call	
1	1	Homophonic; melody in trumpets and trombones against *ostinato* accompaniment pattern in bass; contrasting colors; thin; bassoon, clarinet, and violin embellish.
30	2	Becomes polyphonic; nonimitative; *ostinato* accompaniment continues; fragments presented in contrasting colors.

ARNOLD SCHOENBERG   *Pierrot lunaire*, op. 21, VI: "Madonna"   Side 3, band 8

Polyphonic; nonimitative; solo voice with contrasting accompaniment; flute, bass clarinet, and *pizzicato* cello; each instrument plays individual melody with occasional fusion.

BÉLA BARTÓK   *Music for String Instruments, Percussion, and Celesta*, I   Side 3, band 9

Polyphonic; imitative; violas start with subject; static; thin; entrances continue in blending strings; thickening.

Measure	Call	
1	1	Active pace; major; blending strings; thick; simple harmonies.
4	2	Polyphonic; voices and orchestra in imitation; thick; many strong cadences.
12	3	Homophonic; voices and orchestra in unison melodic line; alternating with block chords.
22	4	Polyphonic; contrasting colors; long-note melody against short-note melody; more complex; thick; sometimes jagged; section ends with strong cadence.
33	5	Homophonic; melody and blending accompaniment; more simple; smooth; becomes thicker; ends with strong cadence.
41	6	Polyphonic; imitative; change in register; more complex; thick texture; ends with half cadence.
51	7	Polyphonic; nonimitative (two contrasting melodies); contrasting colors (women's voices contrast men's voices, and orchestra contrasts voices); repeated ascending patterns; strong cadence.
69	8	Polyphonic; imitative; changes in register; thick; ends with strong cadence.
74	9	Polyphonic; nonimitative (two contrasting melodies); contrasting colors; repeated patterns.
78	10	Mixed texture: polyphonic and homophonic; melody in voices, countermelody in brasses, harmony in orchestra; ends with strong cadence.
92	11	Hymnlike texture in ending cadence.

Measure	Call	
1	1	Homophonic; melody in violins; accompaniment in low blending strings; thin; loud chords punctuate.
7	2	Melody in oboe and violin, then in flute and violin; accompaniment in strings; thickens to deceptive cadence; then to authentic cadence at call 3.
11	3	Melody in low strings; high strings embellish; accompaniment in blending winds; thin.
15	4	Melody in violins; accompaniment in low blending strings; more chromatic; thin.
18	5	Change to minor; melody in violins; accompaniment in blending winds and strings; thicker; strong cadence.
23	6	Melody continues in violins; accompaniment in winds and strings; more chromatic and dissonant; gradual modulation to 7.
28	7	New tonal center; melody in violins; less active; accompaniment in blending strings and winds.
32	8	Melody in violins; accompaniment very thin and smooth.
36	9	Melody continues in violin; accompaniment in strings and winds; thickens; accompaniment becomes more prominent.
39	10	Short phrases in violin, answered by flutes; horns embellish; thin; cadence.

LUDWIG VAN BEETHOVEN   Sonata for Piano in c, op. 13, I (*Pathétique*)

Measure	Call	
1	1	Static pace; minor; thick block chords; pattern repeated; many cadences.
5	2	Homophonic; melody in top part, accompaniment in repeated chords; soft and suddenly loud; thins to cadenzalike melody line.
11	3	More active pace; minor; ***staccato*** in treble against fast repeated octaves in bass; thick; many cadences.
51	4	Less active; treble melody uses ***staccato*** and ***legato***; accompaniment thinner; harmonic pattern repeated.
89	5	More active; many cadences; thickens; strong cadence at end.

Harmony and counterpoint

Measure	*Call*	
1	1	Homophonic; melody in cello; long-note accompaniment changing to shorter notes; smooth; thick; gradual modulation to weak cadence.
12	2	Homophonic and polyphonic; melody in high register (flute and violins); countermelody in cello; harmony in other instruments; more complex.
14	3	Homophonic; sustained chords in blending brass and woodwinds against active violin melody; smooth; contrasting colors.
17	4	Polyphonic; imitative; winds, then low strings; thickens; becomes thinner on downward line; weak cadence.
27	5	Homophonic; melody and contrasting colors in accompaniment; thickens, then thins.
33	6	Melody in winds and strings; harmonic material in *pizzicato* and longer notes; repeated patterns generally thin; becomes thicker briefly.
45	7	Melody lines in strings; woodwinds enter; thick; ends with strong, accented cadence.
49	8	Polyphonic; starts nonimitative, becomes imitative; some harmonic material; contrasting colors and registers; thick; pattern repeated.

Measure	Call	
1	1	Harmonic accompaniment in blending strings; thin; smooth harp chords punctuate; cadence.
15	2	Harmonic accompaniment in blending strings; gradually becomes thicker; flute embellishes.
20	3	Harmonic accompaniment continues in blending strings; simple; thin; cadence.
26	4	Accompaniment begins in blending strings; long notes; then short block chords; thin.
31	5	Pace more active; solo over long sustained note with flute embellishment; then short block chords; thin; section repeated.
49	6	Prominent harmonic accompaniment in blending strings; more complex; thicker, then becomes thinner; cadence.
60	7	Harmonic accompaniment in blending winds; like call 2; smooth.
65	8	Harmonic accompaniment in blending strings; more static; smooth; strong cadence.

Measure	Call	
1	1	Homophonic; minor; thin; repeated harmonic patterns; strong cadences.
23	2	Change to major; accompaniment becomes more prominent; more dissonant; repeated patterns; strong cadence.
31	3	New tonal center; contrasting colors; thinner; smooth.
39	4	Homophonic; thinner; block chords in accompaniment; melody moves downward, accompaniment moves upward.
43	5	Accompaniment more prominent; block chords carry melody; woodwinds embellish; more active; thicker.
49	6	Homophonic; same as call 4.
53	7	Homophonic; same as 3.
61	8	Accompaniment becomes more prominent; block chords rising; density thickens; modulation to 9.
65	9	Original minor key; same as 1.
84	10	Accompaniment more prominent; block chords moving downward; minor; smooth; cadence.
88	11	Major; block chords upward to cadence.

Measure	Call	
1	1	Polyphonic; nonimitative; thin; blending colors in violas and cellos; static pace.
21	2	Homophonic; melody in trumpet; accompaniment in low blending strings; static harmonic rhythm.
31	3	Homophonic; melody in flute; accompaniment in blending strings; thin; remains static.
49	4	Hymnlike texture; blending strings; thicker.
61	5	Homophonic; *pizzicato* melody in low strings; long notes in upper strings; cadence.
64	6	Polyphonic; nonimitative; violins and cellos; thin.
71	7	Polyphonic; nonimitative; long-note melody in violins and cellos against active, short-note melody in violins and violas; thickens.
91	8	Hymnlike texture; full orchestra; thick; some dissonance.
106	9	Homophonic; melody in English horn; accompaniment in low strings; thin; contrasting color.
111	10	Polyphonic; nonimitative; blending colors in horns; static motion.

Measure	Call	
1	1	Trombone solo.
3	2	Bass and **cello** duet over chords in strings; thin; soft.
18	3	Tenor solo; repeated notes in string accompaniment; more active; slightly thicker.
24	4	Trombone enters in duet with tenor; some ⸺⸺.
34	5	Alto solo; string accompaniment; thin; soft.
40	6	Soprano solo; string accompaniment remains the same.
45	7	Short phrases and rising interval of fourth gives effect of slowing up; string accompaniment becomes more sustained.
51	8	Soprano-alto-tenor-bass quartet with orchestra; soft; voices have many rests; ⸺⸺ to loud and ⸺⸺ to ending.

Tone color

Measure	Call	
1	1	Flute; low-middle register; soft.
4	2	Horns have melody; oboe, clarinet, harp, and muted strings accompany; midregister; careful use of silence; thin.
11	3	Flute melody; *tremolo* strings accompany; horns enter; lower register; thin.
14	4	Oboe melody; *tremolo* strings accompany; horns enter; much ◁▷ ; thicker; solo clarinet ends section.
21	5	Flute melody; harp arpeggios; strings accompany; other winds enter at end of section; some ◁▷ .
26	6	Flute melody; strings accompany; midregister; section ends with ▷ .
31	7	Clarinet echoed by flute; horns, harps, and strings accompany; more rhythmic, *pizzicato* in strings.
37	8	Oboe melody; winds and strings accompany; midregister; thicker and ◁▷ .
40	9	Strings and winds echo each other; horns take lead later; all but harps accompany, pushing toward upper register with ◁ .
51	10	Clarinet joined by oboe; strings and woodwinds accompany; descending string line; thin; quiet.
55	11	All winds have same melody; strings accompany; wide range from low to high; much ◁▷ ; thicker.
63	12	Strings take melody; full ensemble accompanies; thick; long ◁ to *ff*, then ▷ .
74	13	Horns, clarinet, and oboe echo; solo violin has countermelody; thin.
79	14	Flute melody; strings in long notes; harp arpeggios; thin.
83	15	Oboe prominent in middle register; more active pace; horns and winds accompany; then descending patterns (*staccato*).
86	16	Oboe melody; soft; strings in long notes; harp arpeggios; thin.
90	17	English horn prominent; harp *glissandi*; horns and winds accompany.
94	18	Low flute solo; solo-violin countermelody; oboe joins; string *tremolo*; antique cymbals lightly.
100	19	Flute with solo cello; winds and harp accompany; ▷ ; thins.
103	20	Oboe melody; strings (ascending), harp, and horns accompany.
107	21	Muted horns and violins; harp and cymbals lightly punctuate; thin; ends with ◁ .

Tone color

Measure	*Call*	
1	1	Loud *pizzicato* chord; oboe and bassoon solo; loud *pizzicato* chords punctuate.
15	2	Pianos and horns prominent; cello enters in high register.
26	3	Alto voices prominent with woodwinds.
33	4	All voices enter; thick; loud.
37	5	Oboe solo; flute accompaniment; thin; soft.
41	6	Alto voices prominent with woodwinds; like call 5; soft but slightly thicker.
48	7	Loud *pizzicato* chord; tenors and sopranos prominent; high register; thick; loud.
52	8	Loud chord; alto and bass voices prominent; low register; getting louder and thicker; moving to higher pitch.
65	9	Thick and very loud; stronger accents in voices against regular accents in accompaniment.
68	10	Thinner; softer.
72	11	Thick and heavy; becoming very loud; all voices, full orchestra.

Tone color

Measure	Call	
146	1	*Fugue subject* in horns, violas, and cellos; wide range; much ⎯⎯ ; many accents.
150	2	*Fugue subject* in violins; horns have countermelody.
157	3	*Fugue subject* in low strings; horns and violins continue with other material.
164	4	*Fugue subject* in tuba and string bass; strings and horns continue in counterpoint.
172	5	*Fugue subject* in high woodwinds; low winds and strings provide counterpoint; thick; loud.
180	6	*Fugue subject* in trombones; other material in full orchestra; character of call 5 continues.
187	7	*Fugue subject* in trumpets; other material continues in full orchestra; thick; loud.
195	8	Trumpets play fragments of *subject*; high register; much overlapping of lines (*stretto*); strings enter with rhythmic pattern at end of section.
212	9	Flute and clarinet melody at two octave intervals; horn holds long note; gradual ⎯⎯ ; thin.
220	10	Melody in English horn; more active than 9; soft.
225	11	Bassoon and oboe duet; thin; soft.
231	12	Counterpoint continues with flute, bass clarinet, English horn, and bassoons.
237	13	Melody in clarinets; other woodwinds enter and drop out; thinning; ⎯⎯ and *ritardando*.
240	14	Melody in unison bass clarinet and bassoon; low register; second melody in muted strings in block chords.
253	15	Flute added to bass clarinet and bassoon; string melody like 14 continues; thickening.
260	16	Melody in unison woodwinds; muted strings continue; thickening; louder; *accelerando*.
273	17	Timpani alone; starts *fff*; ⎯⎯ to *p*; then sudden *fff*; strings in rhythmic figure with strong accents.
285	18	Unison horns in long notes; accents; string figure like 17 continues.
293	19	Horns in dialogue with trombones, string bass, bassoon, and clarinet; string figure like 17 continues; thickening.
301	20	High woodwinds prominent; other material in lower woodwinds, strings, and brass; thick; loud.
317	21	Trumpets prominent; active string patterns; thins.
320	22	Rhythmic dialogue between strings and woodwinds over long note in contrabassoon, string bass, and trombones.
327	23	Dialogue between horns and trombones in long notes; string, brass, and woodwinds in active figures; thick; loud, getting louder; moving to high register.
351	24	Trumpets prominent; loud; horns join in.
354	25	Full orchestra; thick, getting thicker; loud with ⎯⎯ to end.

Tone color

Measure	Call	
1	1	Subject in soprano.
6	2	Subject in alto; countersubject in soprano.
10	3	Episode; new material; action intensifies.
12	4	Subject in tenor; countersubject in soprano.
17	5	Subject in bass (pedal); countersubject in alto; additional counterpoint in soprano.
22	6	Episode; modulates back to main key (g).
25	7	Subject, starting in tenor, suddenly turns into countersubject; subject is resumed in soprano after one-measure hesitation; additional counterpoint in other voices.
30	8	Episode modulates to relative major (Bb).
33	9	Subject in tenor (now in major); countersubject in soprano.
37	10	Episode; repeated pattern; downward.
41	11	Subject in bass (pedal); countersubject in both soprano and alto.
45	12	Episode modulates to subdominant (c).
50	13	Subject in soprano; countersubject (varied) in alto; bass (pedal) with additional counterpoint.
55	14	Episode; lengthy use of repeated pattern; modulates back to original key (g).
63	15	Subject in bass (pedal); fragments of countersubject in soprano; additional counterpoint in other voices; ends with strong cadence.

Measure	*Call*	

Theme

1	1	*A*; piano only.
9	2	*A*; repetition; piano and violin.
17	3	*B*; contrast; piano only.
28	4	*A*; piano and violin.
36	5	*B*; piano and violin.
47	6	*A*; piano and violin.

Variation 1 (primarily *staccato*; piano has primary material; violin accompanies)

1	1	*A*.
1	2	*A*; repetition.
9	3	*B*; contrast.
20	4	*A*.
9	5	*B* ⎫ repetition of calls 3 and 4.
20	6	*A* ⎭

Variation 2 (primarily *staccato*; violin has primary material, moving in small steps; piano accompanies with jagged chords)

1	1	*A*.
1	2	*A*; repetition.
9	3	*B*; contrast.
20	4	*A*.
9	5	*B* ⎫ repetition of 3 and 4.
20	6	*A* ⎭

Variation 3 (*legato*; piano and violin share material; minor key; much parallel motion)

1	1	*A*.
1	2	*A*; repetition.
9	3	*B*; contrast.
20	4	*A*.
9	5	*B* ⎫ repetition of 3 and 4.
20	6	*A* ⎭

Variation 4 (primarily *legato*; violin occasionally *pizzicato*; piano and violin alternate with primary material; major key; mostly small steps)

| 1 | 1 | *A*; piano begins alone; violin enters **pizzicato** in accompaniment. |
| 9 | 2 | *A*; repetition; violin **legato**; piano now has violin accompaniment figure. |

Form · Theme and variations

Measure	Call	
16	3	*B*; contrast; instruments share material; piano *legato*; violin becomes *pizzicato*.
27	4	*A*; piano begins alone; violin enters, becomes *pizzicato* in accompaniment figure.
35	5	*B*; violin has most material; *legato*.
46	6	*A*; violin has primary material; piano has accompaniment figure of 3 and 4.
55	7	Slow; free material; modulating and introducing 8.
62	8	*Coda*; material from the *A* section and new material; quiet cadence ends movement.

Measure	Call	
1	1	Violas start the subject: four short phrases; all strings muted.
4	2	Violins have subject; counterpoint begins.
8	3	Cellos have subject; counterpoint continues.
12	4	Violins have subject; counterpoint continues.
16	5	Basses have subject; counterpoint continues and is extended.
26	6	Violins have subject; imitation in low strings one beat later.
33	7	Fragments of subject in various instruments overlapping in close succession; mutes removed.
40	8	General ◁▷ in all parts; imitative.
45	9	◁▷ continues; complex counterpoint; motion and ◁▷ intensified by call 10.
51	10	Cymbals and timpani roll to 11.
56	11	Climax; strong tonal center; theme in fragmented downward patterns; instruments overlap in imitation; slight *ritardando*.
64	12	Brief overlapping section (*stretto*) as five-note pattern is imitated; downward.
68	13	Violins and violas, one beat apart, with *inverted* (upside-down) subject; counterpoint continues.
72	14	Violins (high register) with *inverted* subject; counterpoint continues.
77	15	Violins (very high) with *inverted* subject; violins (very low) with *original* subject; *tremolo* strings; celeste embellishes.
82	16	Violins, violas, and cellos alternate five-note fragment from *original* subject and *inverted* subject.
83	17	Violins, cellos, and violas further reduce the fragments to three notes, concluding on a unison tonic note.

Measure	Call	
1	1	Passacaglia theme presented in bass (pedal).
10	2	Theme in bass; accompaniment in simple repeated pattern; slight syncopation.
17	3	Theme in bass; accompaniment in simple patterns at lower pitch level; slight syncopation.
25	4	Theme in bass; accompaniment in mostly scalewise motion.
33	5	Theme in bass; scalewise motion continues in accompaniment; more complex.
41	6	Theme in bass — fragmented; accompaniment has wide leaps.
49	7	Theme in bass — now complete; accompaniment in upward scale patterns.
57	8	Theme in bass; accompaniment in downward scale patterns.
64	9	Theme in bass; accompaniment has combination of upward and downward scale patterns.
72	10	Theme in bass — fragmented; accompaniment has repeated skipwise patterns.
80	11	Theme in bass — notes separated; accompaniment has block chords and scalewise patterns.
88	12	Theme in soprano; accompaniment has scalewise runs; no pedal (for first time).
96	13	Theme in soprano; repeated stepwise patterns in pedal; more complex.
104	14	Theme in alto — highly fragmented; often obscure; simple, repeated patterns in accompaniment; no pedal.
112	15	Theme in midbass register — short notes; accompaniment moves by skips; no pedal.
121	16	Theme in midbass and alto — short notes; accompaniment moves upward by skips; no pedal.
128	17	Complete theme in bass (pedal); accompaniment somewhat dissonant; each measure ends with accented chords.
136	18	Theme in bass; accompaniment moves actively in scalewise direction.
144	19	Theme in pedal — fragmented; accompaniment pattern repeats; less complex.
152	20	Theme in bass; accompaniment has short, repeated, scalewise patterns.
160	21	Theme in pedal; short, repeated pattern continues; ends actively with slight *ritardando* and strong cadence.

Measure	Call	
1	1	*First theme* in orchestra; piano accompanies with block chords.
25	2	*First theme* in piano; orchestra accompanies with simple chords.
37	3	*Theme* developed and extended by piano.
60	4	*Theme* in orchestra; piano accompanies with block chords.
77	5	*Theme* fragmented; then transition section.
108	6	Rhythmic motive introduced by piano.
134	7	Motive transferred to orchestra; piano accompanies with arpeggiated-chord pattern.
156	8	Rhythmic motive extended in piano in octaves; transition to call 9.
184	9	*Second theme* in orchestra (winds).
192	10	*Second theme* in piano alone.
204	11	Muted strings play remainder of *second theme.*
218	12	Winds and piano with *second theme*; orchestra accompanies with smooth chordal motion.
235	13	Transition section; piano octaves.
266	14	Strings return with *second theme*; piano takes up downward-chord arpeggio.
291	15	Fragments of *second theme* and rhythmic motive from 6 combined and extended; gradual ———— to full orchestra.
346	16	Transition; piano solo.
357	17	*Second theme* developed in piano.
388	18	Piano and orchestra echo each other with a contrasting motive.
418	19	Rhythmic motive fragmented in winds; piano accompanies.
439	20	Piano repeats rhythmic motive from 8; transition to 21.
471	21	*Second theme* in winds (oboe solo), then strings.
491	22	*Second theme* developed in piano and winds; gradual ———— toward cadenza.
537	23	Cadenza for piano solo; material from 1–23 developed.
607	24	Transition out of cadenza.
612	25	*Second theme* in orchestra, developed and extended.
650	26	*Coda*; strong cadence.

Measure	*Call*	

Exposition

1	1	*Main theme* in tonic (g).
20	2	Repetition with variation; modulation.
28	3	*New theme* used as transition to call 4; contrasting and in major (B♭).
44	4	*Subordinate theme* still in major (B♭).
66	5	*Closing theme*; fragments of *main theme*; still in major (B♭).
		Exposition repeated.

Development

101	6	*Main theme* developed in various keys and instruments.
138	7	*Main-theme* fragment (three-note motive) in thin texture.
152	8	Modulating transition to conclude development.

Recapitulation

164	9	*Main theme* in tonic (g).
183	10	Repetition with variation; modulation.
191	11	*New theme* used as transition to 12; contrasting; major (E♭); extended.
227	12	*Subordinate theme* in tonic (g) instead of major, as in 4.
254	13	*Closing theme* in tonic (g) with fragments of *main theme*.
285	14	*Coda*; strong cadence.

Form · Sonata-allegro

Measure	*Call*	
Exposition		
1	1	*Main theme*: Eb; accompanied by a repeated horn motive similar to theme itself.
9	2	*Main theme* fragmented; extended with woodwind melody.
20	3	Second half of *main theme*; further extension using tail of *main theme*.
29	4	*Main theme* fragmented in transition material.
37	5	*Subordinate theme*: Bb; the quick two-note figure from *main theme* reappears.
44	6	Extension of *subordinate theme.*
48	7	*Codetta*: a phrase and its repetition.
Development		
53	8	*Main theme* used motivically; head of *main theme* and two-note figure prominent, alternating between woodwinds and strings.
64	9	Motivic extension; repetitions.
68	10	*Main theme* fragments; motivic.
Recapitulation		
74	11	Return of *main theme*, as in exposition (Eb).
82	12	*Main theme* fragmented and extended.
98	13	Transition material using *main theme* motivically.
108	14	*Subordinate theme*; now in tonic key (Eb).
115	15	Extension of *subordinate theme.*
119	16	*Codetta*: a phrase and its repetition.

Measure	*Call*	
Menuetto		
1	1	*A* section: g.
	1	Repeated.
15	2	*A'* section; material similar to *A* section but now used imitatively.
	2	Repeated.
Trio		
43	3	*B* section: G; material echoes material of *Menuetto*.
	3	Repeated.
61	4	*C* section.
68	5	*B* section returns; now with horns.
	4 } 5 }	Repeated.
Menuetto		
1	6	Repetition of *A* section; g; no repeat.
15	7	Repetition of *A'* section; ends movement.

Measure	*Call*	

Exposition

1	1	*Main theme*; full orchestra; key of g; first phrase (repeated).
16	2	*Main theme*; second phrase (repeated).
32	3	Extension, which becomes transition.
71	4	*Subordinate theme*; key of B♭; strings introduce phrase repeated by woodwinds.
101	5	Closing material from call 3 presented and repeated.

Development

125	6	*Main theme* fragments given as bridge to development.
134	7	*Main theme* with real beginning of development section; head of *main theme* used motivically and imitatively in strings in dialogue fashion; contrasting registers; modulating extensively.
175	8	Dialogue between lower strings and woodwinds moving to deceptive cadence.
188	9	Closing material on *main theme*, which ends abruptly.

Recapitulation

206	10	*Main theme*: g; first phrase.
214	11	*Main theme*; second phrase.
222	12	Extension, which becomes transition.
246	13	Subordinate theme, now in g (tonic key); strings introduce phrase repeated by woodwinds; full orchestra joining.
276	14	Closing material presented and repeated, then extended to final cadence.

Measure	*Call*	
None	1	First phrase intoned by solo male voice (priest).
	2	Unison male chorus sings three phrases, completing four-phrase structure; mostly one note per syllable.
	3	First phrase again, now with chorus; the entire hymn (four phrases) is then repeated, each time with different words.

Measure	*Call*	
None	1	Monophonic; solo; stepwise (conjunct) motion; narrow range (major sixth, C–A); modal (Dorian).
	2	Unison male chorus repeats "Alleluia" in similar flowing style; melody line extended; no strong rhythmic accent; text predominant; range remains within sixth.
	3	Solo enters with new text; longest phrase of composition; more melismatic; melodic range extended (octave).
	4	Chorus enters on "Dominum," completing melodic movement begun in call 3; smooth contour; mostly stepwise.
	5	Repeat of "Alleluia," like 1.
	6	Chorus enters with material as at 2; leads to modal cadence.

Measure	*Call*	
None	1	*A* section; two-part nonimitative polyphony (note against note style); unaccompanied; melody in upper voice; added lower voice begins in unison moving stepwise to interval of a fourth below the melody, then returning to unison; thin; no meter but even beat; one note per syllable; slight pause at end of phrase provides cadence feeling.
	2	*A* section: call 1 repeated with different text.
	3	*B* section; new melody in upper voice (fifth above starting pitch of opening section); added lower voice begins in unison moving stepwise to interval of a fourth below the melody then returning to unison; thin; no meter but even beat; one note per syllable; slight pause at end of phrase provides cadence feeling.
	4	*B* section: music of 3 repeated with different text.

Measure	Call	
None	None	Solo voice; male countertenor (high tenor); monophonic; modal; smooth; mostly small steps; narrow range; mostly triple meter patterns, trochaic (*1-2*-3) with occasional iambic (1-*2-3*); strong cadences.

Measure	Call	
1	1	Two voices; textless upper voice "ah" has long, smooth, mostly stepwise melody against lower voice singing cantus-firmus text in long notes; suggestion of triple meter; narrow range.
20	2	Descending melisma in quicker notes in upper voice; freer; less metrical.
23	3	*Clausula* section (lower voice now is in measured rhythm but still has longer notes than upper voice) on syllable "om-."
29	4	Return to opening style as in call 1; upper part in free, unmeasured movement; wider range.
35	5	Final cadence moves from dissonant interval to unison.

Measure	Call	
1	1	$\frac{6}{8}$ meter; modal; three rhythmically contrasting voices; lowest part has three-note rhythmic motive (♩.♩.│♩.𝄽) that occurs throughout first half (up to call 3); middle voice has alternating long and short notes; upper voice is syllabic in mostly even notes; overlapping phrases among the parts.
20	2	All three parts come to a close, then continue in style of 1.
33	3	Lowest part and middle voice now in same rhythm; upper voice continues as before; persistent rhythmic patterns throughout piece; vertical sounds have a hollow quality, especially at cadences; *ritardando* to suspension (dissonance) and final cadence.

Measure	*Call*	
1	1	*a* section (refrain); contralto voice, lute, and vielle in nonimitative polyphony; triple meter; distinct phrases in voice parts separated by rests; mostly short notes against long notes of bowed vielle; plucked lute notes give rhythmic emphasis to bowed vielle part; refrain ends with strong cadence.
23	2	*b* section; new melody idea; continues in character of call 1; mostly small melodic steps; short phrase structure continues in voice; ends on half cadence.
23	3	*b*: section at 2 repeated; new text.
1	4	*a*: section at 1 repeated; new text.

Were the composition to continue, there would be additional text and it would proceed as follows: *a b b a a b*. . . .

Measure	Call	
None	1	Drum introduction; regular beat; buysine (trombone) fanfare; leads to call 2.
	2	*a* section; rebec (bowed string) and tenor violin; large leap followed by narrow, stepwise melody; drum continues; two-note buysine fanfare separates sections.
	3	*b* section; rebec, then sopranino recorder, then recorder and tenor violin take up new melody in style of section *a*; tambourine accompaniment.
	4	*a*: repeat of 2.
	5	*c* section; rebec and recorder play tune; tambourine continues accompaniment.
	6	*a*: repeat of 2.
	7	*b*: repeat of 3.
	8	*a*: repeat of 2.
	9	*c*: repeat of 5.
	10	*a*: repeat of 2, followed by short codetta.

Measure	Call	
1	1	*a* section (refrain); duple meter; two-part imitative polyphony; melismatic vocal line over longer note instrumental tenor part played by viola da gamba; vocal line moves mostly by steps; thin.
8	2	*b* section (stanza); new melody with the same characteristics as call 1; solo range extended; becomes more melismatic at end of section.
8	3	*b*: stanza; music of 2; new text.
1	4	*a*: refrain; music of 1; new text.
1	5	*a*: refrain repeated (words and music).

Measure	Call	
None	1	*a* section; drum introduction; duple meter; polyphonic; active pace; pardessus de viole and lute exchange melodic material over slower moving part played by tenor violin; all parts *pizzicato*; melodic material is composed of short fragments of repeated syncopated rhythm (♪♪ ♪♩); half cadence.
	2	*a*: repeat of call 1; short extension, ending with full cadence.
	3	*b* section; continues in the style of 1 and 2; duple meter continues to be supported by active drum beat.
	4	*a*: 1 and 2 repeated (minus drum introduction).
	5	*b*: 3 repeated.
	6	*c* section; short codetta or postlude in triple meter; drum fades to end piece.

Measure	Call	
1	1	*a* section (introduction); $\frac{6}{8}$ meter; active pace; regular beat; bassoon; recorder and violin in imitation; strong cadence.
6	2	*a* continued: single instruments double voices; imitative; narrow range; frequent crossing of parts; strong cadence; short instrumental interlude leads to call 3.
15	3	*b* section; new melody; imitation continues between upper and lower voices; similar texture to section *a*; imitative instrumental postlude with strong cadence.
1	4	*a*: repeat of *a*; stanza 3 (*a* always includes introduction and interlude, as in 1 and 2).
1	5	*a*: repeat of *a* as in 1 and 2; stanza 4.
1	6	*a*, *b*: return to 1 for repeat of *a* and *b* (1–3); stanzas 5 and 6.
1	7	*a*, *b*: return to 1 for repeat of *a* and *b* (1–3); stanzas 7 and 8.

Measure	*Call*	
1	1	Nonimitative polyphony in bass and countertenors (alto part); triple meter; mostly small steps; consonant; transposed Dorian mode with major sound; very melismatic; strong cadence.
13	2	Sopranos and tenors enter to complete four-part texture; soprano in strict canon with alto at distance of a sixth; tenor in strict canon with bass at distance of a sixth; new voices (soprano and tenor) sing the music from call 1 at different pitch level; thicker; more complex; strong cadence.

Measure	*Call*	
None	1	Soft drum and tambourine provide introduction; triple meter; strong beat; viol enters with melody; modal; narrow range; strong cadences.
	2	Melody of call 1 repeated in viol; recorder and lute in octaves; tambourine continues.
	3	New melody; viol; tambourine continues.
	4	Melody of 3 repeated in viol; recorder and lute in octaves; tambourine continues.

Measure	Call	
1	1	Imitative polyphony; duple meter; voices often heard in pairs; mostly stepwise; constant changes in thickness (one voice, two voices, three voices).
16	2	All four voices now heard together; many overlapping cadences.
19	3	Two lower voices immediately imitated by upper two voices; frequent imitation continues among all four voices.
29	4	Deceptive cadence; rhythm becomes less complex; mostly even notes; imitative entries continue in all four parts; strong cadence.
42	5	Change to triple meter; imitation continues in mostly stepwise motion; cadence.
58	6	Return to duple meter; rhythm becomes more complex; four-part texture predominant; final cadence has hollow sound although more traditional triads were heard in internal cadences.

Text	*Call*	
La bel'Aronde . . .	1	*a* section (refrain); homophonic; major; six voices; fast; irregular beat; rhythm of music governed by rhythm of text; strong cadences; consonant harmonies at ends of phrases; faster and slower sections alternate.
Gentile Aronde tu viens . . .	2	*b* section; new section; less active; longer notes; minor; more chromatic.
La bel'Aronde . . .	3	*a*: repeat of refrain (call 1).
Quand nou quitant tu depars . . .	4	*b*: repeat of 2.
La bel'Aronde . . .	5	*a*: repeat of refrain (1).

Measure	*Call*	
1	1	Imitative entrances successively in first *cantus, altus*, second *cantus* (strict canon of first *cantus*, tenor, and bass; first-*cantus* (and second-*cantus*) melody descends stepwise followed by octave leaps upward; additional counterpoint continues in other voices.
10	2	First and second *cantus* continue in canon; descend stepwise through distance of octave; other parts provide additional counterpoint.
18	3	First and second *cantus* continue in canon; stepwise patterns with occasional skips; imitative entries follow in *altus*, tenor, second *cantus*, and bass; opening pattern of call 3 reappears later, modified after first six notes.
33	4	Smooth, ascending four notes form melodic pattern that permeates entire section; entrances in first *cantus*, tenor, second *cantus* (canon with first *cantus*), *altus*, and finally bass; much counterpoint in other parts.
42	5	Elaboration and extension of melodic motive of 4.

Measure	Call	
1	1	*a*; short, narrow-range motive treated in imitation; modal; duple meter; active pace; regular, strong beat; density quickly expands to four parts; cadence.
14	2	*b*; new, short melodic fragments in pairs of instruments; immediately imitated and repeated several times; echo effects.
28	3	*c*; cadence; change to triple meter; new upward motive; some subtle syncopation; imitation in pairs; density varies.
45	4	*d*; change to duple meter; new short syncopated motive treated in ongoing imitation; density more constant than call 3.
49	5	*c*: repeat of 3.
66	6	*d*: repeat of 4.
71	7	*a*: repeat of 1; conclusion at end of this section.

Measure	*Call*	
None	None	Vocal ensemble (soprano, alto, tenor, and bass); duple meter; static pace; regular, weak beat; short, smooth melodies treated with some imitation; cadence points obscured by overlapping phrases; free, or "through-composed," form, in which new melodic ideas are introduced with each new line of text.

Measure	Call	
1	1	Five-part unaccompanied chorus; upper parts move mostly stepwise while bass provides downward harmonic movement; thick; half cadence followed by short section in chordal style.
9	2	Text changes; imitative three-part texture; thinner.
12	3	Text changes again; return to five-part chordal texture.
20	4	Strong cadence in minor followed by sustained chordal section; strong cadence in major.
32	5	Text changes; successive two-, three-, and four-part texture in contrapuntal style.
39	6	Return to more sustained chordal style; thicker; strong cadence in major.
49	7	Text changes; contrapuntal section using two distinct motives: one ascending, the other descending in stepwise motion; pace quickens slightly to strong cadence in major.

Measure	Call	
1	1	Triple meter; regular beat; melodic interest in treble; simple texture; many strong cadences.
5	2	Short points of imitation using opening notes of melody in call 1 can be heard several times at different pitch levels.
13	3	Melody in style of 1; mostly stepwise and downward; strong cadence at end.
21	4	Shorter note values predominant; both steps and skips; bass becomes active at end of section; strong cadence.

Measure	Call	
1	1	Section 1; sopranos and altos in imitation; static; smooth; duple meter; weak beat; modal (Aeolian); cadence overlapped by call 2.
8	2	Section 2; tenors, basses, and sopranos in imitation; many steps with some leaps; thicker; strong cadence overlapped by 3.
17	3	Section 3; all four voices in ongoing imitation of short "head themes"; some pairing of voices; more complex; generally shorter notes; much descending motion.
24	4	Section 4; soprano introduces new text "Dona nobis pacem" ("Give us peace"); four-part imitation continues; many suspensions; strong cadence at end with picardy third (major third).

Measure	*Call*	
1	1	Solo voice accompanied by organ and bass lute; recitativelike rhythm imitates the natural accents of the text; mostly small steps in short melodic fragments; slow changes in harmonic accompaniment; no regular beat.
8	2	Same melody repeated with rhythmic alterations to fit the words.
13	3	Melody changes direction to depict word "tornare" ("to return").
14	4	Pace slows considerably to depict word "rimango" ("remain").
25	5	Leap of a fourth upward to depict word "stelle" ("stars").
31	6	Melodic line falls to depict "morte" ("dead").
34	7	Melody rises when text speaks of "cielo, e sole" ("heaven, and sun").

Measure	Call	
1	1	Instrumental introduction: duple meter; regular beat; minor; begins homophonic with melody in first cornettino; rising scale patterns and some skips up and down in bass (harpsichord and cello); becomes more imitative in cornettino parts; narrow range in wind instruments; simple rhythm patterns.
18	2	First tenor enters with first-cornettino melody from call 1; cornettinos decorate vocal line in short imitative phrases.
23	3	Second tenor enters in imitation of first tenor; cornettinos continue to decorate as in 2; first tenor now provides counterpoint for second tenor; some dissonance; thicker; strong cadence.
37	4	Cornettinos drop out; voices move in parallel motion; second-tenor phrase treated in imitation; smooth return to homophonic style.
49	5	Second-tenor phrase from 4 becomes basis of imitation between cornettinos and voices.
54	6	New melodic idea; alternating imitation between voices and instruments; much parallel motion; small steps; narrow range; ♩♫ pattern predominant.
65	7	After final statement in voices of melodic idea from 6, notes become shorter in both voices and instruments; action becomes more complex and intensifies; *ritardando* to strong cadence in major.
74	8	Instruments alone (*Sinfonia*); homophonic; dotted patterns predominant; less active and complex than 7.
82	9	Voices enter in close imitation; cornettinos provide additional counterpoint; bass line in downward motion; *ritardando* to strong final cadence.

Measure	*Call*	
1	1	Slow; four upper string parts supported by continuo (harpsichord and cello); thick; many dotted rhythms; continuo bass keeps repeating opening four-note figure; very modulatory (going through C, D, and G); full cadence.
1	2	Repeat of call 1.
11	3	More active pace; meter change; new musical idea; imitative; more tonal (primarily on C); more complex; strong cadence.
27	4	Return to meter and tempo of 1; more homophonic; tonality of C continues throughout section.
11	5	Repeat of 3 and 4.

Measure	*Call*	
1	1	Continuo (harpsichord and cello) plays descending chromatic ground bass; triple meter; static; long notes; rhythm and pitches of ground continue throughout aria though often with varying harmonies above it.
5	2	Soprano enters over repetition of ground; strings provide harmonic accompaniment; solo melody uses small steps with two downward skips (both on word "trouble").
15	3	Repetition of call 2.
25	4	Soprano has new melodic figure over same ground; shorter phrases, higher register than 2 and 3; more complex and chromatic harmony in instruments provides intensity for climax (highest notes repeated on words "remember me"); final cadence.
36	5	Repeat of 4.
47	6	Last two statements of ground with many suspensions and rapid chord changes in strings.

Measure	Call	
1	1	Introduction of one measure of descending arpeggios; descending sequence in keyboard figures in fast-note, dance-type patterns; longer, even notes; single, low sustained note in pedal; duple meter.
5	2	Free imitation based on parts of ascending and descending minor scale against slow-moving pedal notes; some ornamentation.
14	3	New imitative material based on broken-chord (arpeggiated) figure; pedal continues in slow, sustained notes; imitation of ideas continues to final strong cadence.

Measure	*Call*

Movement I

None   1   Static pace; duple meter; two violins in imitation; lyrical; wide range; continuo (organ and cello) provides harmonic accompaniment; numerous suspensions (dissonant sounds) are quickly resolved to consonances; modulates to dominant, then returns to tonic for strong final cadence.

Movement II

None   2   More active pace; duple meter; cello participates in contrapuntal texture; many sequential passages and sequential modulations; suddenly slow for strong final cadence.

Measure	Call	
1	1	*Main melody*; triple-meter feeling; imitation in bass; much ornamentation in melody; cadence.
5	2	*Main melody* repeated; slight modification at the cadence.
1	3	Calls 1 and 2 repeated.
8	4	Same as 1 except *main melody* now higher (in different key).
11	5	*New melody*; nonimitative; quickly cadences in major; gradual modulation back to original key with use of *main melody* from 1.
11	6	Repeat of 5.

Measure	Call	
1	1	*A*: *tutti* (full ensemble); duple meter, regular beat; major; thick; loud; simple consonant harmonies; cadence.
5	2	*B*: *soli* (two flutes and continuo of harpsichord and cello); sudden shift to c; soft; continuo drops out (treble strings accompany); contrasting thin texture.
9	3	*A*: *tutti*; thick; loud; like call 1.
13	4	*C*: *soli*; imitation; modulatory; becomes homophonic before strong cadence in G.
23	5	*A*: *tutti*; new tonal center (G); thick; loud; strong cadence.
28	6	*D*: *soli*; starts with ascending scales in imitation; modulates to e; strong cadence.
37	7	*A*: *tutti*; new tonal center (e); thick; loud; strong cadence.
41	8	*E*: *soli*; fast notes in parallel thirds; trills; modulation to a; strong cadence.
50	9	*A*: *tutti*; new tonal center (a); strong cadence.
54	10	*F*: *soli*; mostly fast notes in imitation; modulation to C.
65	11	*B*: *soli*; like 2; sudden shift to c; continuo drops out; strong cadence in C.
70	12	*A*: *tutti*; final statement; slowing to full cadence.

Measure	*Call*	
1	1	*Introduction*: strong beat; active pace; soft; high melodic line against contrasting bass line; strong cadences.
7	2	Homophonic; melody in soprano; soft; medium range; harmonies slightly embellished in higher strings; thin; generally smooth chord motion.
12	3	Tenor voices enter in imitation (polyphony); soprano melody continues in long phrases against short fragments in tenor; stepwise; spins out; still soft; simple chords support counterpoint.
18	4	Alto voices enter in imitation; bass voices enter and continue; long phrases; stepwise; spins out; simple chords support counterpoint; remains soft.
30	5	Voices merge separate strands; dotted-note pattern prominent; gets louder.
33	6	Solid chords in voices (homophony); loud; simple, consonant chord structure; string accompaniment embellishes with stepwise patterns; thick.
37	7	Voices return to polyphony; tenor voices enter and continue against short phrases; stepwise; spins out; simple chords support counterpoint; thinner.
49	8	Solid, block chords in voices; loud; like call 6.
53	9	Voices return to polyphony; short phrases; alto voices enter and continue; stepwise; spins out; smooth modulation to subdominant (from G to C); simple chords support counterpoint.
65	10	Voices merge separate strands; like 5; dotted-note pattern predominates.
68	11	Solid, block chords in voices; loud; like 6; smooth modulation back to tonic.
73	12	Thickens; beat remains steady; upper voices and strings continue in long, stepwise motion; spun-out embellishment against short phrases in lower voices.
79	13	Voices merge separate strands; like 10; dotted-note pattern predominates.
85	14	Solid, block chords in voices; like 11; section ends with strong cadence.
91	15	*Instrumental coda*; uses previous melodic material; simple; steady beat; high melodic line against contrasting bass line; *ritardando* to strong cadence.

Measure	*Call*	
1	1	*Instrumental introduction*; major; triple meter; active pace; regular beat; strong accents; ♪♫ rhythm prominent; scalewise passages with frequent skips; strong cadence at end.

A section

22	2	Voice enters with motive from introduction on word "Perfido!"; cello and harpsichord provide thin, simple accompaniment for bass solo; occasional loud interruptions by orchestra in higher register; long melismas on extended vowels; section ends with longest melisma.
67	3	Several alternations of full orchestra echoed by voice.
78	4	"Perfido!" motive in orchestra; long, sustained note in voice against more active orchestral accompaniment; immediately followed by long melisma.
93	5	Alternation of orchestra and voice; similar to call 3; voice ends with strong cadence.
105	6	Active instrumental section; loud; similar to material heard throughout work; ends with strong cadence in tonic key.

B section

118	7	Change to minor; shorter and more modulatory than *A* section; voice and continuo predominant; isolated loud interruptions in orchestra with "Perfido!" motive; section ends with sudden slow cadence in minor.

A section

149–265	8	Exactly the same as calls 1–6. This constitutes the *da capo*, the return to the beginning.

Style · Baroque   **66**

Measure	*Call*	
1	1	Entire section, calls 1–13, uses imitative polyphony; *chorale melody* presented in tenor and viola; countermelody in cello; major; thin.
6	2	*Chorale melody* presented in alto, voice, and orchestra; tenor continues with counterpoint; long phrases; mostly stepwise; spins out; cello continues with countermelody.
11	3	*Chorale melody* presented in soprano, voice, and orchestra; tenor and alto continue with counterpoint; cello continues with countermelody; thickening.
16	4	*Chorale melody* presented in bass voices and orchestra; other voices continue with counterpoint; long phrases; mostly stepwise; spins out; cello continues countermelody; thick and very active.
23	5	Trumpet enters with *chorale melody* in longer notes; high; continuo instruments enter in bass (bassoon and organ) with *chorale melody*; voices and strings continue in active counterpoint; trumpet embellishes at cadence.
32	6	*Chorale melody* now in soprano; alto has counterpoint; cello returns with countermelody; thinner; regular beats.
37	7	Bass enters with *chorale melody*; alto and soprano continue counterpoint; cello continues countermelody; trumpets embellish.
42	8	Tenor enters with *chorale melody*; counterpoint in other voices; countermelody continues in cello; thickening.
48	9	Trumpet enters with *chorale melody*; active counterpoint in other voices and orchestra; continuo bass returns; section ends with long pedal point in continuo to strong cadence.
60	10	*Chorale melody* in tenor; thinner; cello returns with countermelody; other voices enter gradually as in opening section; long phrases; mostly stepwise; spins out; thickening.
82	11	Same as 5.
91	12	*Chorale melody* in soprano; other voices enter gradually in imitation; cello returns with countermelody; thickening.
107	13	Same as 9.

Measure	*Call*	
1	1	Minor; triple meter; static, two-note pedal point in bass (short, repeated, stepwise motive); contrasting soprano melody enters with line curving upward and downward; numerous ornaments.
13	2	Gradual modulation to major; bass continues with two-note pedal point; repeated stepwise motives both upward and downward; soprano has long, mostly stepwise melody; spins out; much ornamentation; gradually moving to lower register.
27	3	Short modulation back to minor; bass continues with two-note pedal point; repeated stepwise patterns; upward and downward; soprano has steps and large leaps; more jagged; section ends with elaborate embellishment on major chord.
45	4	*Short coda*; continues in character of call 3; cadence at end with long ornamentation; extended dissonance finally resolved.

Measure	Call	
1	1	One-measure introduction; strings and bassoon; simple "clock" rhythm; violins have **main theme**; material from introduction continues as accompaniment; thin; static; consonant; strong cadences; structure of 5 measures + 5 measures.
	1	Repeated.
11	2	Alternation of loud and soft; rhythmic accompaniment continues; dotted rhythm prominent; **legato** and **staccato** combined; mostly smooth, stepwise motion.
24	3	Returns to **main theme**; flute now reinforces violin melody; rhythmic accompaniment continues; simple harmonic structure; some ——◁ ▷——.
34	4	Sudden shift to minor; loud; new melodic material; dotted rhythm prominent; steady beat; thicker; contrasting colors; pitch range moves higher; regular accents.
50	5	Return to major; violins have downward melodic pattern; syncopated; rhythmic accompaniment continues; full orchestra; dotted pattern present in woodwinds; section ends with simple harmonic structure over extended pedal point; then violin has two-note pattern that leads to call 6.
61	6	Return to **main theme**; thinner; higher; solo bassoon plays rhythmic accompaniment; violin has melody; flute and oboe embellish; dotted rhythm becomes prominent; cadence.
	6	Repeated.
97	7	One-measure rest; **main theme** presented in new major key; rhythmic accompaniment continues in strings; violin plays variation of **main theme**; flute embellishes; contrasting; gradual transition in violin to 8.
111	8	**Main theme** in original key; rhythmic accompaniment returns; flute and violin play melody; more ornamented; increased pitch range; trumpet and timpani added; repeated triplet pattern in accompaniment; thicker.
125	9	Fragments of **main theme**; ▷—— *p*; rhythmic accompaniment continues; running-note pattern continues in accompaniment; rather active; gradually thinner.
135	10	*Coda*; **main theme**; *ff*; further embellished; regular accents; simpler harmony; section ends with downward scale passages; thinner; ▷—— to pedal point in low strings; quiet cadence.

Measure	*Call*	

Exposition

1	1	*Theme 1*; strings only; major; *legato* and *staccato*; thin.
9	2	*Theme 1* in full orchestra; loud and thick.
19	3	*Theme 2*; combination of short and long notes; thick; cadence material moves to half cadence.
36	4	*Theme 1* in imitative polyphony; thin; *legato* and *staccato*; regular pulse; then full orchestra, joined by call 5.
56	5	*Theme 3*; imitative polyphony; modulating; trills and dotted rhythm prominent; thick.
64	6	*Theme 2*; extended; thick; cadence.
74	7	*Theme 4* in violin with *theme 3* in bassoon and *theme 2* in flute; then flute and bassoon echo each other with *theme 3*; thin; imitative.
94	8	*Theme 4*; imitative; generally ascending; dissolving into active, scalewise, descending figures; thick and loud.
115	9	Extension material (end of *theme 1*); generally ascending; modulating; thick; active; accents.
135	10	*Theme 2* (imitative); given exact and inverted in strings, altered in woodwinds; oboe and then bassoon close section with *theme 2*.

Development

| 158 | 11 | *Theme 1* heard twice at opening, but *theme 2* is primary material; altered and reworked; frequently interrupted by beginning of *theme 1* in altered notes; contrasting colors; regular beat; alternating thick and thin densities; thins to bassoon and violins with *theme 2* as preparation for recapitulation. |

Recapitulation

225	12	*Theme 1*; tonic key; *legato* and *staccato*; melody in strings; woodwinds play harmony; thin.
233	13	Development of *theme 1*; melody in violins; mostly small steps; lower strings and woodwinds embellish; long and short notes.
253	14	*Theme 3* (trill and dotted rhythm) moving to *theme 2* as extension material to half cadence; thick.
272	15	*Theme 4* in tonic key; *theme 3* in bassoon; *theme 2* in flute; becomes *theme 3* in flute and oboe with *theme 3* in bassoon; thinner.
292	16	Development of *theme 4*; imitative; thick; both long and short notes; modulatory; gradually dissolves into transition material from end of *theme 1*; generally ascending; strong cadence.
334	17	Extension and closing material; *theme 2* altered and reworked; moves to strong cadence which leads onward to coda.

Measure	Call	
Coda		
360	18	Brief transition material; thin; long notes; *legato*.
372	19	All four themes now appear in contrapuntal texture (concentrate on hearing all the themes as they appear).
408	20	Cadential extension using material from *theme 2*; strong cadence in full orchestra.

Measure	Call	
1	1	Full orchestra; active pace; major; regular accents; suddenly soft; then ———— to half cadence.
17	2	Two voices (Leporello, bass, and Don Giovanni, baritone) enter in alternation; active accompaniment in orchestra; voice parts use both leaps and steps; simple harmonic structure; many cadences.
47	3	Change to $\frac{6}{8}$ meter; new melodic idea in winds of orchestra (represents supper music played by offstage orchestra); simple harmonies; regular accents; bass and baritone sing comments; many cadences.
118	4	Change to $\frac{3}{4}$ meter; accompaniment continues in winds; new tonal center; simple harmonies prevail; melodies are narrow and simple in construction; smooth modulation to call 5.
162	5	New tonal center; change to duple meter; new dotted-rhythm motive (borrowed from Mozart's own *Marriage of Figaro*); balanced phrases; simple, balanced structure.
183	6	Accompaniment becomes more complex with the introduction of downward scale runs in clarinets; *Figaro* motive from 5 repeated at end.
200	7	Change to triple meter; more active pace; Donna Elvira (soprano) sings downward melodic pattern against rising bass motive in orchestra.
223	8	Soprano solo now has upward, leaping patterns; accompaniment less complex; bass and baritone soloists added; all three voices continue to intertwine; accompaniment becomes more complex and thicker as Donna Elvira concludes and exits.
348	9	Orchestra continues with rising chromatic motives; strong accents; Elvira screams; chromatic motive continues as Don Giovanni and Leporello investigate.
362	10	Chromatic motive continues; Leporello screams; ———— and thickening to brief half cadence and pause.
379	11	Change to duple meter; vocal solos in short phrases over long pedal point (long note) in horns; strings maintain beat with active repeated patterns.
433	12	Loud, dissonant, thick chords in orchestra; bass (now the Commendatore) and baritone soloists enter in alternation; jagged, light, violin countermelody; some syncopation; less active pace; some accents.

Measure	*Call*	

Scherzo (*A*)

1	1	Active pace; fast; triple meter; thin; mainly strings; *staccato*; short, even ♩♩♩ melodic pattern; *scherzo theme* in violin and oboe; steady beat; consonant.
31	2	Chromatic pattern leads to modulation; *theme* repeated in strings and flutes in new key; regular accents; sudden shift to *pp*; texture thins to one note; then thickening and ◁— to call 3.
93	3	Full orchestra with *scherzo theme*; thick, regular accents; combination of *legato* and *staccato*; simple harmonic structure; *staccato* continues.
115	4	Syncopation with strong accents, echoed by quiet block chords in regular pulse; simple two-note pattern echoed between winds and strings; gradual ◁— to *ff*.
	2–4	Repeated.

Trio (*B*)

166	5	French horns have *triadic theme*; upward motion; theme is in contrast with the *scherzo theme*; repeats.
199	6	*New theme*; contrasting colors; downward motion; unison *legato* wind pattern repeated and extended by strings.
225	7	French-horn *triadic theme* again, altered at end of phrase; some *sf* —▷ ; pace slows; *rubato*; repetition of downward patterns.
	6, 7	Repeated.

Scherzo (Varied *A*)

255	8	Return to *scherzo theme* in strings and oboe; *staccato*; downward motion in melody; steady pulse (♩♩♩).
286	9	Chromatic pattern leads to modulation; *theme* repeated in strings and flute in new key; regular accents; texture thickens, thins to single note, then thicker and ◁— to 10.
350	10	Full orchestra with *scherzo theme*; thick; regular accents; simple harmonic structure.
373	11	Syncopation with strong accents echoed by quiet block chords; *staccato*; two-note echo pattern; gradual ◁— and strong cadence pattern.
423	12	*Coda*; deceptive change to *p*; timpani maintain steady pulse; ◁— to short conclusion with strong cadence.

Measure	Call	

Exposition

1	1	*Main motive*: E♭; unison; strong *ff*; no beat implied yet.
6	2	*Main motive* imitated and extended in strings; more active pace; steady beat; starts soft; ——— to block chords; violin held note suspends motion.
22	3	*Main motive*; unison; slightly higher than call 1; *ff*.
25	4	*Main motive* imitated and extended in strings; ascending; active pace; steady beat; regular accents; modulatory; starts soft; thickens and ——— to 5.
45	5	New tonal center (c); *main motive* is imitated and extended by strings; descending woodwinds have harmonic accompaniment; thick; strong cadence.
59	6	*Motive* in solo horn.
63	7	*Theme 2*; more lyrical; imitated in strings and woodwinds; soft; thin.
83	8	*Theme 2* extended in repetitive pattern; thickening and ——— to 9.
94	9	Full orchestra; *new melodic idea* in violins; active; winds play block-chord accompaniment on first beat of measure, then shift to second beat.
110	10	Strong descending pattern; major; strong cadences halt movement.

Development

125	11	*Main motive* stated in horn and clarinet; strings answer.
129	12	*Main motive* developed in strings; winds play harmonic accompaniment; modulatory.
146	13	*Main motive*; more fragmented; motive downward and inverted (upward); winds eventually take up development.
155	14	*Main motive* inverted in alternation between strings and winds; ——— to 15.
165	15	Full orchestra; loud; thick; use of rests.
179	16	*Main motive* developed and fragmented; combination of *legato* and *staccato*.
196	17	Two-note fragment of *motive* echoed between strings and winds; then to one-note fragment of *motive*; ——— to *pp*.
240	18	Sudden *ff*; *main motive* used in transition to recapitulation.

Recapitulation

248	19	*Main motive*: E♭ unison; strong *ff*; no beat implied yet.
253	20	*Main motive* imitated and extended in strings; more active pace; steady beat; starts soft; ——— to block chords; violin held note suspends motion.
268	21	One-measure cadenzalike extension by oboe.
270	22	*Main motive* imitated and extended in strings; ascending; active pace; steady beat; regular accents; modulatory; starts soft; thickens and ——— to 23.
288	23	New tonal center (c); *main motive* is imitated and extended by strings; descending woodwinds have harmonic accompaniment; thick; strong cadence.
303	24	*Motive* in solo horn.
307	25	*Theme 2*; more lyrical; imitated in strings and woodwinds; soft; thin; key is now C.

Style · Classic   **74**

Measure	Call	
331	26	Four-note fragment from **theme 2**; extended repetitive patterns; thickens and ▷ to 27.
350	27	Full orchestra; **new melodic idea** in violins; active winds play block-chord accompaniment on first beat of measure, then shift to second beat; active.

Coda

375	28	Extension of three-note pattern from **main motive**; thick; loud; full orchestra.
398	29	Fragments of **motive** extended in lower strings; timpani embellish; starts **legato**; then combination of **legato** and **staccato**; section ends **staccato**.
439	30	Fragments of **motive** echoed by strings and winds; more static.
480	31	**Main motive** in full orchestra; extended in strings; woodwinds have accompaniment.
491	32	**Motive** in tonic (E♭); repeated; thick; soft and suddenly loud; strong cadences end movement.

Measure	*Call*	

Exposition

1	1	**Theme A**: key of C (tonic); heavy and marchlike; duple meter; full orchestra; steady beat; thick; active; section ends with descending, scalewise passages in strings and woodwinds; accents on offbeats.
26	2	**Theme B**; more *legato*; longer notes; melody in horns changing to strings; steady beat; theme serves as transition and modulation to call 3.
44	3	**Theme C**; second important theme; key of G (dominant); strong, regular beat; alternating loud and soft; upward and downward; ———— to end of section; two block chords; half cadence.
64	4	*Closing theme*; key of G (dominant); starts thin; blending strings and woodwinds; becomes thicker; change to minor (a) at end of section; full orchestra.

Development

90	5	**Theme C**; key of A; fragmented; steady beat; thinner; contrasting colors (strings and woodwinds); modulatory.
110	6	**Theme C**; lengthened and presented in triplet figure (♩♩♩ ♩ | ♩♩♩ ♩); triplet figure in bass embellishes; contrasting colors; **theme B** in long upward movement in strings.
132	7	Continuous **tremolo** in strings; winds then take up ascending motive dissolving into thick, loud, repetitive cadence material.
154	8	Sudden quiet; **new theme** (from movement III); key of C (tonic); triple meter; thin; static pace; woodwinds prominent; section ends with ———— to recapitulation.

Recapitulation

207	9	**Theme A**; key of C (tonic); duple meter; full orchestra; heavy and marchlike; steady beat; thick; active; section ends with descending scalewise passages in strings and woodwinds; accents on offbeats.
231	10	**Theme B**; more *legato*; longer notes; melody in horns changing to strings; steady beat; theme serves as transition and modulation to 11.
253	11	**Theme C**; now in key of C (tonic); strong, regular beat; alternating loud and soft; upward and downward; ———— to end of section; two block chords; half cadence.
273	12	*Closing theme*; still in C (tonic); starts thin; blending woodwinds and strings; ———— and thickening in transition to 13.
294	13	**Theme C**; used as two motives: triplet figure and four-note figure as countermelody; gradually ascending to thick block chords; half cadence.

Coda

| 318 | 14 | **Another new theme** (unexpected for coda); less active pace; contrasting colors; starts thin; thickens and ———— to cadence; *accelerando* to 15. |

Style · Classic   **76**

Measure	Call	
362	15	*Presto* section; primarily cadence material; accents; thickens and ———— to 16.
405	16	Full orchestra; 40 measures of strong chords in final cadence.

Measure	*Call*	
A section		
1	1	**Theme A**; key of G (tonic); triple meter; melody in violin against harmonic accompaniment in lower strings; regular beat; many quick ◁══▷ used throughout movement.
	1	Repeated.
9	2	Contrasting melody; regular beat; ranges extended; some ◁══▷ ; strong cadence.
17	3	**Theme A**; change of register; steady beat; some ◁══▷ .
	2, 3	Repeated.
B section		
25	4	**Theme B**; melody in violin against active string accompaniment; more polyphonic; wider range; louder; more *staccato*.
41	5	**Theme B** in cello and viola; new tonal center (C); active string accompaniment; combination of *legato* and *staccato*.
57	6	Motivic development of **theme B**; fragmented and modulatory; combination of *legato* and *staccato*; some *rubato*.
A section		
81	7	**Theme A**; key of G (tonic); higher register; soft.
89	8	**Theme A**; ornamented in violin; active; wide range; static accompaniment in lower strings; section extended.
121	9	**Theme A**; melody in first violin; second violin has countermelody.
Coda		
130	10	Fragments of **theme A**; thin; modulatory; section ends with pause.
141	11	False return of **theme A**.
143	12	**Theme A** leads to final cadence in G (tonic).

Measure	*Call*	
1	1	Introduction: single-note triplet figure in treble against less active ascending pattern in bass; minor; single-note treble ♪♪♪ pattern expands to thicker texture; some *rubato*; ◁◁▷▷ ; half cadence.
7	2	Voice enters over half cadence; cadence resolves on last note of opening phrase; ♩.♪ prominent; triplet and bass figures from introduction serve as accompaniment for solo; smooth; short phrases; dramatic ◁◁▷▷ ; strong cadence; short piano transition to call 3.
16	3	Change to major; accompaniment continues in triplet pattern as before; bass in long notes; solo phrases now longer; much *rubato*; cadence with pause.
23	4	Minor; accompaniment changes to block chords; less active; solo continues in smooth phrases to cadence in minor.
27	5	Phrase repeated with altered ending to cadence in major; piano transition to 6.
31	6	More active pace; major; solo in shorter phrases; both leaps and steps; repeated accompaniment patterns.
38	7	Sudden change to minor; accompaniment from 6 continues against long notes in solo.
40	8	Change to major and from $\frac{4}{4}$ to $\frac{6}{8}$; more active; ♩♪ pattern prominent; section ends with repeated sequences in voice and accompaniment; sudden hold and *rubato* at cadence stops motion; piano transition in $\frac{4}{4}$ to 9.
58	9	Repeat of material from 3.
64	10	Moving downward to low range; voice and accompaniment in octaves; less active; accompaniment expands to block chords; strong cadence in major; piano plays short, final cadence.

Measure	Call	
1	1	Polyphonic; imitative; major; active pace; strong beat; *legato*; brass chords punctuate with syncopated figure.
21	2	Winds enter with *first theme*; contrasting colors; *staccato* and *legato*; syncopated figure in all winds; ends with repeated downward scale passages punctuated with high upward flourishes.
37	3	Alternating patterns of *ff* and *p*; chromatic and ascending; beat remains steady; *first theme* reappears in imitation at end of section.
65	4	Brass in loud block chords answered by soft repeated pattern in string and woodwinds; repeated four times at different pitch levels.
88	5	Fragments of *first theme* developed imitatively in *pizzicato* bass and winds; accompaniment in string *tremolo*; thin; ——— to call 6.
107	6	*New theme* (Dies Irae) announced in low horns and cellos; accented long notes; *first theme* in violas; thin; less active pace.
123	7	*First theme* treated in imitative polyphony in strings; constant roll of timpani; woodwinds added; gradual ——— and ascending; thickening to 8.
154	8	Chords in offbeat accents (syncopation); *ff*; thick.
174	9	*First theme* in strings; active pace; *ff*; winds then add contrasting *Dies Irae theme* (long notes against short notes of *first theme*); *first theme* dissolves into fast scales in high woodwinds and strings; *Dies Irae theme* continues *ff* in other winds.
204	10	Abrupt change of texture; upward short patterns and flourishes; repeated patterns on wooden part of bow (*col legno*); winds play embellished thematic fragments (trills).
220	11	Woodwinds alone; *staccato*; loud chords in full orchestra; some *pp* ——— *ff*; modulates back to opening tonal center; section ends with rapid patterns in strings with brass chords.
245	12	Repeated accompaniment pattern of *tremolo* ——— in strings and timpani; *Dies Irae theme* fragmented.
256	13	*Coda* in full orchestra; loud and thick; repeated cadence patterns drive to strong final cadence.

Measure	*Call*	
Introduction		
1	1	Accented octave in bass followed by rapid, repeated pattern in bass; minor key.
Section *A*		
5	2	Florid pattern in treble; steps and leaps; very chromatic; repeated accompaniment pattern continues in bass at various pitch levels; subtle ◁= ◁══ ; section ends with *ritardando*.
25	3	Material from call 2 repeated; subtle ◁══ to *f*; accompaniment pattern stops at beginning of chromatic line in treble; downward interlude; *ritardando* to Section *B*.
Section *B*		
37	4	New tonal center; less active pace; repeated triplet pattern in bass; treble melody in long, smooth, ornamented phrases; much *rubato*; some ◁= ══▷ ; melody repeats in long arcs of movement.
Section *A*		
49	5	Like 2; florid patterns in treble; steps and leaps; wide range; very chromatic; repeated accompaniment pattern continues in bass at various pitch levels; subtle ◁= ══ ; section ends with *ritardando*.
68	6	Material from 5 repeated; subtle ◁══ to *f*; accompaniment pattern stops at beginning of chromatic line in treble; downward interlude; *ritardando* to 7.
Coda		
80	7	Repeated pattern in treble; bass accompanies in octaves; general downward direction.
84	8	Repeated pattern in bass and treble; gradual *ritardando*; thinning and ══▷ to 9.
92	9	Pattern in treble only, then single-note restatement of *B section* melody in bass; soft; thin; *ritardando* to two block chords as final cadence.

Measure	*Call*	

Section *A*

1	1	(*a*) Triple meter (waltz); *theme 1* in first violin; major; stepwise; other string instruments accompany in *pizzicato* chords on second beat.
12	2	Repetition of *theme 1* in all violins; higher register; countermelodies in accompaniment; louder; more homophonic.
19	3	(*b*) *Theme 1* extended; oboe and bassoon in octaves; strings accompany in *pizzicato* chords; thinner.
28	4	Clarinet repeats extension as in call 3; more *rubato*; punctuated chord accompaniment.
37	5	(*a*) Return of *theme 1*; clarinet and bassoon in octaves; low register; broken-chord accompaniment in strings.
44	6	Repetition of *theme 1* in higher register by woodwinds; ⟩ ; *legato*; ascending countermelody; thicker; small steps.

Transition section

| 57 | 7 | *Theme 2* in bassoon; *rubato*; wide range; *pizzicato* chords accompany. |
| 64 | 8 | Repetition of 7; theme now in woodwinds in octaves. |

Section *B*

72	9	(*a*) *Theme 3*; minor and modulatory; violins *spiccato* (bouncing bow); mostly stepwise melody is spun out; much ⟨══ ; thin.
80	10	Repetition of 9 in violas; lower register; accompaniment *legato* and thicker.
88	11	(*b*) Extension of *theme 3* fragmented; alternating colors; frequent shifts in dynamics; combination of *legato* and *staccato*; patterns repeated over and over.
124	12	(*a*) Return of *theme 3*, as at 9 in violins and at 10 in violas; mostly stepwise; retransition to section *A*.

Section *A*

149	13	(*a*) *Theme 1* returns in oboe; tonic key; violins use *staccato* motive from *theme 3* in accompaniment; thin.
153	14	All violins repeat *theme 1*; higher register; accompaniment thicker; more homophonic.
161	15	(*b*) *Theme 1* extended; oboe and bassoon in octaves; strings accompany in *pizzicato* chords; thinner.
169	16	Clarinet repeats extension, as in 15; more *rubato*; punctuated chord accompaniment.
178	17	(*a*) Return of *theme 1*; clarinet and bassoon in octaves; melody repeated in higher register by all woodwinds; string accompaniment changes from broken chords to *legato* small-step rising movement; ⟨══ .

Measure	*Call*	

Transition section

| 198 | 18 | ***Theme 2***; bassoon; wide range; ***rubato***; ***pizzicato*** chordal accompaniment. |
| 205 | 19 | Repetition of 18 in all woodwinds; higher register. |

Coda

213	20	Closing section; violins with ***new theme***; chromatic; *p* ——— *ff*; thick chordal accompaniment; soft string cadence.
228	21	Repetition of 20; cadence.
241	22	***Motto theme*** from movement I, but now in triple meter in clarinet and bassoon; shifts between soft and loud; ends suddenly with six loud chords in full orchestra.

Measure	Call	
1	1	*Main theme* in low strings; *ff*; thick chords in winds and brass; mostly short notes; theme repeated at lower pitch; chords repeated at higher level.
5	2	Piano enters with ascending pattern in octaves; repeated; mostly short notes; orchestra punctuates with loud chords.
10	3	Piano cadenza; thick block chords upward and downward; *rubato*.
14	4	*Main theme* developed; *accelerando* and general upward direction in rapid, repeated patterns; *ritardando* to call 5.
24	5	Trumpet fanfare over piano trill in low register; rapid ascending pattern and ⏤⏤⏤ to 6.
27	6	*Main theme* in strings; thin wind chords punctuate; steady beat; thin; soft; piano enters; beat stops; much *rubato*.
34	7	*Main theme* in strings; higher pitch than 6; thin chords in winds punctuate; piano enters; beat stops; thick block chords; then rapid single-note descending pattern with subtle ⏤⏤⏤ .
44	8	Less active pace; piano outlines chord structure; clarinet obbligato in wide range; ⏤⏤⏤ ; piano embellishes melody; section serves as transition to 9.
50	9	*New melody* idea in piano; answered by clarinet; more active pace.
56	10	*Melodic idea* (9) repeated by piano at higher pitch; answered by violin.
62	11	Piano extends idea, cello and clarinet enter with countermelody.
67	12	More active pace; steady beat; *main theme* fragmented in bassoon and cello; other strings and winds accompany; piano arpeggiates; general thickening and *accelerando*; ⏤⏤⏤ to 13.
73	13	*Main theme* in full orchestra; fast; loud; piano enters; orchestra punctuates with block chords.
81	14	Piano develops *main theme*; descending half-step patterns in octaves; mostly short notes; orchestra punctuates with block chords; *ritardando* to 15.
90	15	Piano in thick block chords; both upward and downward; *rubato*; ⏤⏤⏤ ; cadence.
94	16	*Main theme* in bassoons; slower; strings and winds accompany; steady beat; piano enters; beat stops; *rubato*; thin; both long and short notes.
99	17	*Main theme* in strings; steady beat; piano enters; much *rubato*; low strings accompany in sustained block chords; ⏤⏤⏤ ; piano alone in descending single-line patterns; *ritardando* to 18.
107	18	*Main theme* in violin; steady beat; accompaniment in lower strings; piano arpeggiates; bassoon takes up stepwise countermelody; some ⏤⏤⏤ .
113	19	Arpeggios continue in piano; clarinet countermelody; winds and strings punctuate with block chords.
117	20	Piano begins ascending half-step patterns; winds and strings hold block chords; ⏤⏤⏤ ; quiet, quick cadence ends movement.

Measure	*Call*	
1	1	Orchestral introduction; triple meter; major; static pace.
5	2	Chorus enters; sopranos have long, smooth melody; other parts provide blending counterpoint; some ═══ ═══ ; strong cadence; brief orchestral interlude.
17	3	Chorus enters; *legato*; ═══ ═══ continues; beat remains steady; section ends with strong cadence.
25	4	Tenors enter with long, smooth melody; soft; thin; basses enter in imitative polyphony, then sopranos and altos; ═══ and thickening; strong cadence; short orchestral interlude ends section.
47	5	Voices in chorale style, then basses enter with melody; more jagged; tenors, altos, and sopranos enter in imitation; ═══ and general upward motion to *f*; then ═══ to call 6.
59	6	Voices in chorale style against short notes in accompaniment; smooth modulation and strong cadence in new tonal center.
66	7	Material from 2 developed; combination of homophonic and polyphonic; modulatory; much ═══ ═══ ; accents in accompaniment; strong cadence in tonic key; orchestral interlude to 8.
90	8	Return to opening melody; like 2.
102	9	Phrase like 3, but more polyphonic.
112	10	Voices in octaves; smooth countermelody in orchestra; soft; thin.
116	11	Voices in block chords; countermelody continues in orchestra; general ═══ .
124	12	Double fugue; *subject 1* in long notes in soprano against short notes of *subject 2* in bass, then in alto and tenor; counterpoint becomes more fragmented and leads to section with voices in chorale style against short notes in orchestra; soft.
155	13	Coda: fragments of opening phrase from 2 in octaves; some ═══ ═══ .
165	14	Texture becomes more polyphonic; two lines; gradual ═══ and thickening to *f*; then ═══ to strong cadence in tonic key.

Measure	*Call*	
1	1	Tenor solo in long, smooth, upward phrases; flute obbligato parallels melody; homophonic; $\frac{6}{8}$ meter; static pace; major; accompaniment in *pizzicato* strings; thin.
14	2	Short interlude in woodwinds; tenor solo returns in long, smooth phrases; cello, oboe, and bassoon parallel voice; accompaniment in winds.
20	3	Strings in long notes and *tremolo* added to accompaniment; voice continues in long, smooth phrases; broadening ———— and thickening to *f*; voice alone at climax of phrase; much *rubato*; orchestral accompaniment returns and modulates to call 4.
29	4	Return to melody of 1; cello and bassoon obbligato parallel voice; accompaniment in *staccato* strings and *legato* woodwinds.
42	5	More active pace; voice sings repeated-note pattern, then changes to long, smooth line; ———— and thickening to *f* and held high note; then downward smoothly.
49	6	Pace becomes less active; then solo has upward repeated-note patterns to held high last note; ———— to *pp*.

RICHARD WAGNER   *Tristan und Isolde*: "Liebestod"

Measure	Call	
1	1	Homophonic; major; slow; static pace; soprano solo in smooth, short phrases; blending harmonic accompaniment in strings (*tremolo*) and winds; general ———> .
9	2	Accompaniment becomes more prominent; more active pace; harp arpeggiates; solo line in continuous, smooth phrase; wide range; ——< .
12	3	Soprano solo more prominent; smooth; short phrases like call 1; accompaniment thinner; less complex; general *accelerando*; some ——>——< .
16	4	Accompaniment more prominent; many countermelodies; melody embellished by solo clarinet, oboe, and flute; soprano solo is continued in long, smooth phrases.
27	5	Dramatic leaps highlight melodic line; accompaniment in strings (*tremolo*); winds have countermelodies; harp embellishes; much ——>——< .
36	6	Accompaniment becomes thinner and less complex; soprano solo has stepwise pattern; generally upward; ——>— and thickening.
42	7	Accompaniment more prominent; soprano solo in long phrases; both upward and downward; dramatic contrasts of louds and softs in orchestra; harp embellishes.
56	8	Soprano solo in smooth, upward phrases; accompaniment in winds and strings (*tremolo*); much ——>——< ; generally ascending; *accelerando* and thickening to 9.
60	9	Climax on long note in high register; pace then becomes less active; general thinning and ——> ; voice has smooth, interrupted phrases against countermelodies in orchestra; harp embellishes.
67	10	Sudden change to minor and end of vocal solo; some ——>——< ; return to major for quiet orchestral ending.

Measure	*Call*	
1	1	*Theme A*; arpeggiated in solo oboe; harp and muted strings accompany; static; thin; complex harmony.
3	2	*Theme B* in solo flute; chromatic; descending line; harp and strings accompany; flute solo leads to whole-tone chords.
8	3	*Theme C* in clarinet; stepwise; dotted pattern prominent; harp and strings accompany with descending chords.
12	4	Flute takes over and embellishes *theme C*; higher range; harmonic accompaniment becomes more complex; texture thickens; ◁━━━ ; harp and celesta embellish with arpeggios.
17	5	Meter changes; parallel, descending chords in harp, celesta, and strings; *legato*; thin.
18	6	Flute duet; smooth; woodwinds provide harmonic accompaniment; harp embellishes with arpeggios; subtle ◁━━▷ .
22	7	Oboe solo uses material from call 6; woodwinds accompany; harp arpeggiates.
23	8	Sudden *f*; thick; full orchestra; arpeggios in harp and celesta; fast scales in woodwinds; gradual thinning and ━━▷ .
28	9	*Theme D*; oboe solo; chromatic; dotted pattern prominent; strings, horns, and harp provide harmonic accompaniment.
32	10	Sudden *f*; thickening and ◁━━ ; strings take *theme D*; move to higher register; complex texture.
36	11	Sudden *p*; *theme B* in high flute and celesta; harp arpeggios.
38	12	Oboe takes *theme B*; harp arpeggios.
39	13	Flute and then bassoon repeat *theme B*; strings have *legato* stepwise pattern; gradually moving higher; harp arpeggios.
43	14	Thickening and ◁━━ to *ff*; intensity increases greatly; then gradual ━━▷ and thinning to 15.
48	15	*Theme B*; solo violin; high register; repeated pattern in harp accompanies; thin.
50	16	Blending flutes and clarinets; static; soft; thin.
51	17	*Theme C*; solo clarinet; muted *legato* string accompaniment.
55	18	*Theme C* continued in solo flute; accompaniment in divided strings; harp and celesta embellish.
58	19	Gradual move to cadence; ━━▷ and thinning; dissonant, weak cadence chord is held.
61	20	Like 1; *theme A* arpeggiated in solo oboe; harp and muted strings accompany; static; thinning to final cadence on whole-tone chord (indecisive).

Measure	*Call*	
1	1	Blending strings; very slow and soft; weak beat; violin melody moves in stepwise phrases; much *rubato*; slow harmonic rhythm; strong tonal center; some ⬍ ; section ends with half cadence.
8	2	Melody continues in long, smooth, even stepwise notes; introduction of melodic leap upward; echoed by lower strings; theme then transferred to viola; accompaniment in blending strings; violins continue with countermelody; some ⬍ ; *rubato*; smooth modulation to half cadence.
19	3	New tonal center; viola has melody; starts with long, smooth, even stepwise notes; leaps become more prominent; slight — to call 4.
23	4	Dissonance between top and bottom; > *p*; viola carries melody; gradual modulation back to original key.
28	5	Original key; smooth, stepwise melody in cello; blending string accompaniment; intensity gradually increases; *p* < *mf*; leaps become larger.
40	6	Melody in first violins; activity continues to increase; overall move toward higher register; cello melody line in upper register; ⬍ .
44	7	Melody in second violins; general upward direction continues; melodic lines begin to overlap; < to *ff*; climax of work; very intense; high notes to sudden silence.
53	8	Sudden shift to *pp*; return to middle register; section ends with perfect cadence; silence.
57	9	Repetition of original melody; like 1; first violin and viola have melody; gradual > ; ends in major; cadence pattern repeated an octave lower to long note fading to end.

Measure   *Call*

1   1   Duple meter; active pace; strings and woodwinds with repeated figure; horns enter with fanfare melody; trumpets join later; steady beat; regular accents.

18   2   Repeated figure stops; low strings repeat horn-fanfare figure; winds added; contrasting colors; irregular meter; strings play long *tremolo*; general upward movement in winds; strong accents; thickening and ⟨ ——— ⟩ to call 3.

37   3   Return to repeated figure in strings and woodwinds; horns and trumpets prominent; other instruments added; ⟨ ——— ⟩ to 4.

43   4   Strong accent; less active pace; softer; strings play static, *legato*, harmonic accompaniment; long, smooth, continuous melody in cello; winds embellish; texture thickens; much *rubato*; ⟨ ——— ⟩.

59   5   Thin; soft; contrasting colors and registers; various woodwinds play fragments of melody; strings have simple harmonic accompaniment.

66   6   Repeated stepwise pattern in flute serves as accompaniment for new melody (from movement II) in oboes and clarinet; thin; soft; static; bassoon joins flute at end of section.

74   7   *Pizzicato* in lower strings; timpani embellish; marchlike; irregular accents; regular beat; horns enter with new fanfare melody; low register; alternates with bassoon trio.

94   8   Strings take over marchlike figure of bassoons from 7; tuba and string bass with repeated-note figure on offbeats; brasses play fanfare melody; trumpets enter with melody from movement II now in fanfare style; *tremolo* strings and timpani accompaniment.

108   9   Woodwinds and horns take up fanfare melody; string-and-timpani accompaniment continues.

114   10   Woodwinds and trumpets prominent with fanfare melody; range extended; string-and-timpani accompaniment continues.

120   11   Melody (from movement I) in strings, trumpet, and piccolo; thick; loud; clash in rhythm between long and short figures.

131   12   Horns and trumpets prominent; active treatment of fragments from 11; contrasting colors; thick; much ⟨ ——— ——— ⟩ ; *rubato*; strong accents and ⟨ ——— ⟩ to 13.

149   13   Less active pace; long, smooth, lyrical melody (from movement I) in strings; high register; harp and timpani prominent; duple meter; thick; loud; very intense; leads to dramatic pause.

161   14   String quartet with material from movement I; thin; soft; static; gradually thickening; ascending melody line in strings; becomes marchlike with syncopation; moves to thick, repeated material over long drum roll; trumpets prominent with idea from 11 in different rhythm; pause.

181   15   Brasses play final, slow statement of melody from movement II; loud; final chord ⟨ ——— ⟩ .

Measure	*Call*	

Introduction

| 1 | 1 | Duple meter; loud; active; ——— . |

Section *A*

| 4 | 2 | ***Theme A*** in upper winds; brass plays harmonic accompaniment; ***staccato***; soft; thin; modal; irregular phrase length (9 measures + 4 measures). |
| 17 | 3 | Suddenly loud; *theme A* in upper winds and trumpets; ***staccato***; loud; thicker (full band); irregular phrase length (9 + 4). |

Section *B*

| 31 | 4 | Less active pace; ***theme B*** in woodwinds and trumpet; long, smooth, clear-cut phrases; accompaniment in offbeat patterns; alternates between major and minor; soft; thin; balanced 8-measure phrases; strong cadences; some ═══════ . |

Section *C*

| 64 | 5 | Change to $\frac{6}{8}$ meter; low brasses have long-note theme against active, ***staccato*** theme in woodwinds and percussion; thick; loud; active; balanced 8-measure phrases; strong cadences. |
| | 5 | Repeats. |

Section *B*

| 91 | 6 | Same as call 4. |

Section *A*

| 1 | 7 | Same as 1 and 2. |
| 17 | 8 | Suddenly loud; like 3; strong sudden ending in major with dissonance. |

Measure	Call	
1	1	*First verse*: repeated pattern in piano (*ostinato*); different repeated *pizzicato* patterns in violin; flute *legato*; contrasting colors; steps and leaps in voice; wide range; *Sprechstimme* (song-speech) style of singing; atonal.
11	2	Instrumental interlude; polyphonic; some imitation; jagged; wide range; thin; mostly *legato*.
18	3	*Second verse*: soft; *ostinato* pattern from call 1 divided between all instruments; thin; irregular, weak beat; both long and short notes.
23	4	Voice range more narrow; polyphonic accompaniment continues; *staccato* and *pizzicato*; soft and thin; general ══ and slowing.
28	5	*Third verse*: louder; thicker; combination of polyphonic and chordal texture; piano and cello in unison; meter shifts; voice range wider; *ritardando* to call 6.
35	6	Sustained *legato* notes in strings; flute embellishes with rapid descending pattern; *ostinato* pattern from 1 in bass of piano.
39	7	Final statement of *ostinato* in piano and then flute, ending the song.

Measure	Call	

I

| 1 | 1 | No beat; no tonal center; nonimitative polyphony in short, interrupted spurts; combination of long and short notes; contrasting colors with unusual use of instruments; sparse, thin texture; wide leaps from pitch to pitch; wide range; subtle ⟩⟨ ; celesta trill. |

II

| 1 | 1 | More active than movement I; no beat; nonimitative polyphony continues in short phrases; soft; wide range; nonrepeated fragments in winds and solo violin; mixture of wide leaps and small steps; *ritardando* to triangle roll. |
| 9 | 2 | Polyphonic fragments of shorter duration; chordal sounds lead to trumpet fanfare with ◁ to sudden end. |

III

1	1	Repeated notes in harp, guitar *tremolo*, and roll in percussion instruments serve as accompaniment for static, jagged, violin melody; timpani added; thinning; ▷ and *ritardando* to call 2.
4	2	Horn solo; wide range; percussion accompaniment now in short spurts.
6	3	More active; clarinet and then violin have spurts of jagged melody against *pizzicato* accompaniment; some ◁▷ .
8	4	Return to repeated-note pattern like 1 serves as accompaniment for jagged trombone solo; subtle ◁▷ ; ends with soft timpani roll; thinning and ▷ ; snare-drum rolls in spurts.

IV

| 1 | 1 | Mandolin, then trumpet, and then trombone have short, jagged, melodic fragment; clarinet repeated-note and sparse chord accompaniment; repeated notes in different instruments lead to final melody fragment in violin. |

V

1	1	Glockenspiel melodic line; strings have chords; trumpet and then oboe carry melodic line forward.
5	2	Viola solo; jagged; wide range; spurts of percussion instruments and cello lead to loud climax.
10	3	Nonrepeated fragments in horn, violin, and clarinet against accented chords; *tremolo* in pitched percussion instruments; ◁ and *accelerando* to climactic *fff* accented chords.
18	4	Melodic line distributed among celesta and harp and cello and oboe; soft; static.

Measure	Call	
26	5	Tiny pitch fragments shift from instrument to instrument leading to long viola pitch and two final chords.

Measure	*Call*	
1	1	Short introductory figure in cornet and trombone; marchlike ground-bass figure in duple meter begins; cornet, trombone, bassoon, clarinet, and violin have short melodic fragments; thin; mostly short notes.
30	2	Material continues above bass figure; irregular meters; frequently interrupted by rests and jagged solo fanfares; sparse orchestration; mostly short notes; dotted-note figure prominent but disappears toward end of section; some dissonance.
50	3	All instruments play same melody and rhythm; contrasting colors easily distinguished; bass figure obscured by shifting meters and syncopation; dissonant; thinning to bass figure.
64	4	All winds in syncopation above bass figure; shifting meters continue; high register; contrasting colors easily distinguished; strong irregular accents.
84	5	Thinner; bassoon repeats dotted-note figure; drum beats lead to weak, syncopated final cadence.

Measure	Call	
1	1	Strong offbeat accents in march rhythm provides accompaniment for jagged trombone solo.
10	2	Cornet plays jagged, *staccato* melody; accompaniment of dissonant, syncopated, sparse chords and repeated drum beats.
22	3	Jagged bassoon solo interrupts; ═══ to call 4.
26	4	Cornet solo again; short notes become *legato* in smoother line in each instrument.
39	5	Short melodic spurts; shifting meters; strong, irregular accents; thin; much contrast among colors.
60	6	Static bassoon melody; stopping and starting; thin.
67	7	Cornet repeats first part of jagged, *staccato* melody several times, then completes it; other instruments enter in nonimitative lines; irregular meters and irregular accents continue.
92	8	Fanfare; drum prominent; strong accents; upward *glissandi* in trombone.
97	9	Violins and clarinet prominent; shifting meters; both long notes and short notes; syncopation; then trombone takes up melody from 1; accompaniment in offbeat accents.
107	10	Cornet melody returns interrupted by bassoon solo; trombone followed by cornet with variation of bassoon melody; clarinet embellishes.
130	11	Trombone repeats melody from 9; strong offbeat accents in accompaniment; sudden cadence ends movement.

Measure	Call	

Section *A*

| 1 | 1 | Violin solo accompanied by percussion; strong, distorted tango rhythm; violin (which echoes material of an earlier piece) plays dissonant, jagged double stops and melody in interrupted fragments; shifting meters; generally static with short bursts of more active material; clarinet enters at end. |

Section *B*

| 34 | 2 | New material interrupts; clarinet in low register with repeated figure; violin melody; shifting meters. |

Section *A* continuation

| 41 | 3 | Continuation of material of call 1; violin solo accompanied by percussion in strong, distorted tango rhythm; clarinet joins in weak cadence on long notes to end section. |

Measure	*Call*
1	1	Hymnlike; chorale style (both homophonic and polyphonic); violin and bass begin in ***tremolo***; highest melody is most prominent with other voices moving along together in subordinate role; many complete phrases ending with full cadences; some cadences followed by long-note "echo"; generally dissonant and unblending; ***legato***; dissonant chords; ends with full "Amen" (plagal) cadence, which is consonant; reminiscent of Bach's "Ein feste Burg" chorale, but completely modern in expressiveness.

Measure	Call	
Introduction		
1	1	Short figure in low *pizzicato* strings; duple meter; active pace.
Exposition		
6	2	*Motive A*: strong tonal center (C); unison strings now with bow; mostly short notes in small steps; ascending and descending motion; prominent rhythm pattern with pick-up note.
18	3	Piano plays varied repetition of *motive A*; irregular accents; mostly short notes; timpani interrupt; short melodic fragments are treated in imitation and inversion (upside down); complex texture; ═══ to timpani cadence; pause.
68	4	Soft; jagged line; thinner; repeated in imitation in higher and lower register; all strings; mostly regular accents; thickens; ═══ .
94	5	Suddenly soft ascending line; many strong irregular accents; long ═══ to call 6.
110	6	Successive trill; much ═══ ═══ ; percussion accents; material gradually ascends to high register; thickens and becomes more jagged and complex with overlapping lines; high and low; then thins and ═══ to 7.
155	7	Melody stated in piano; then restated in variation by low strings; dissolves into two-note motive (*glissando*); ═══ to strong syncopated cadence in G.
Development		
182	8	Timpani introduce even-note material (like *motive A*) that is taken up by piano and *pizzicato* strings; this serves as accompaniment for melody in strings, harp, piano, and xylophone; much syncopation; complex texture; ═══ to 9.
242	9	Episodic section; less active; soft; all *pizzicato*; imitative; many changes in meter; irregular accents; ═══ ═══ ; high harp has repeated figure; material descends to low register with short recurrence of two-note motive from 7; descends further to static string and timpani figure.
309	10	*Fugue*: section begins in low cello; very chromatic; timpani accompany; shifting meters and irregular pulse; gradually thickens and ascends; ═══ ; section ends with repetitions of the beginning of the subject; descending and *ritardando* to ═══ ; pause.
Recapitulation		
373	11	*Motive A*: thick; active pace; mostly short notes in small steps; much ascending and descending motion; slowing and thinning to short fragments; much overlapping and imitation.
400	12	Repetition of material from 4 in waltzlike meter; thin; soft; piano embellishes with ascending chromatic passage at end.
428	13	Three-note downward motive; getting faster; *glissando* at end and pause.

Style · Twentieth century   99

Measure	Call	
449	14	Closing material; thick; strongly accented; complex texture; long *glissandi*; short motives; speeding and slowing; uses material from entire movement; strong cadences emphasize C key feeling.

Time	*Call*	
0.00	1	Fragmented statement of melody; echo between trumpet and bongo; weak pulse becoming strong.
0.15	2	Trumpet improvisation on melody; narrow range; no harmonic accompaniment; regular pulse.
0.30	3	Trumpet improvisation on melody; narrow range; harmonic accompaniment added; repeated rhythm in accompaniment.
1.00	4	Guitar improvisation on melody; running-bass accompaniment; irregular accents; regular pulse; repeated rhythm in piano accompaniment.
1.59	5	Piano improvisation on melody; wide range; complex; jagged; running bass; regular pulse; cymbals in repeated patterns.
2.58	6	Alto-saxophone improvisation on melody; wide range; complex; jagged; running bass; regular strong pulse.
4.25	7	Fragmented improvisation on melody as follows; sax, drums, trumpet, drums, sax, drums, trumpet, drums, sax, drums, trumpet, and drums.
5.08	8	Alto-sax improvisation on melody; low register; regular pulse; fade out; $\Longrightarrow$; bongo alone at end.

Time	*Call*	
0.00	1	Introduction: strings; very small steps; very dissonant throughout; narrow range; blending colors; slow; thin; no pulse; some ⟨⟩ .
0.27	2	Alto-saxophone solo; long notes; large leaps; accompaniment thicker; some ⟨⟩ ; percussion sounds; no pulse; cymbal added.
1.45	3	Alto sax continues; long notes; large leaps; some ⟨⟩ ; increased activity in accompaniment; increased percussion activity; unchanging texture goes on and on.
2.55	4	Increased percussion activity; no pulse; cello duet, then in unison with solo sax; long notes; cymbal ⟨⟩ .

Time   *Call*

0.00   1   Introduction: piano; bass accompaniment; thin; steady pulse; blending brasses in syncopation; echo in blending woodwinds; *ostinato* pattern; piano returns.

0.31   2   Statement of melody; unison saxophone and fleugelhorn; long notes; wide range; smooth; accompaniment thicker; steady pulse; ⸺ to *sfz*; thick brass accompaniment; some ⸺ in accompaniment; clarinet embellishes; solo out; interlude; thick block chords in brass; irregular accents; solo back; accompaniment thickens; ⸺ to *sfz*; fleugelhorn embellishes; irregular accents in accompaniment.

1.55   3   Second statement of melody; blending woodwinds; thinner; trombones embellish; brass accompaniment; flute embellishes, then to solo in flute; accompaniment thin; brass accompaniment becomes thicker; irregular rhythmic accents; ⸺ .

3.04   4   Third statement of melody; sax and fleugelhorn; long notes; wide range; smooth; accompaniment thick; ⸺ to *sfz*; fleugelhorn embellishes; accented brass chords; woodwinds blending; trombones embellish; brass accompaniment ⸺ .

4.09   5   Ending: active flute solo; brass block chords in irregular accents; steady pulse; descending line to sudden cadence.

Time	*Call*	
0.00	1	Introduction: major; brass in chorale harmony; narrow range; trumpet solo; regular pulse; repeated accompaniment pattern (**ostinato**); irregular accents; soft to loud.
0.30	2	*Theme 1*: vocal solo; short phrases; regular pulse; **ostinato** pattern; thick chordal accompaniment.
1.07	3	Interlude: **ostinato** pattern; loud to soft.
1.15	4	Repetition of **theme 1**; vocal solo; accompaniment thicker.
1.52	5	Interlude: **ostinato** pattern; loud to soft; thicker texture.
1.59	6	*Theme 2*; vocal solo; faster tempo; accompaniment thickens; ═══ ══ ; *ritardando*; cadence.
2.27	7	Repetition of **theme 1**; vocal solo; regular pulse; **ostinato** pattern; thick accompaniment; voice alone.
3.02	8	Interlude: tempo more active; piano solo; repeated **ostinato** and rhythmic patterns; texture thickens; ═══ .
3.15	9	Trombone improvisation on **theme 1**; high; strong beat; **ostinato** pattern in piano.
3.42	10	Trumpet improvisation on **theme 1**; regular pulse; **ostinato** pattern; **ostinato** stops; **ostinato** returns.
4.00	11	Alto-saxophone improvisation on **theme 1**; wide range; accompaniment thin; **ostinato** stops.
4.08	12	Two trumpet improvisation on **theme 1**; wide range; accompaniment thickens; **ostinato** returns.
4.18	13	*Theme 2* returns; vocal solo; suddenly slower tempo; more static pace; thicker texture; ═══ ; organ cadence.
4.45	14	Repetition of **theme 1**; solo voice; harmonica embellishes; voice alone.
5.23	15	Like introduction; major; brass in chorale harmony; narrow range; trumpet solo; solo voice enters; ═══ to cadence.

Time	*Call*	
0.00	1	Percussive sound of string players striking the body of instruments with their hands; combination of short and long sounds; no beat; irregular rhythms; woodblock plays once.
0.35	2	Violins bowed; cello *pizzicato*; percussion sounds continue; alternation of *pizzicato* and use of bow in all strings; irregular spurts of sound and rhythm; motion gradually increases and thickens; woodblock adds to intensity; sudden pause.
1.40	3	*Pizzicato* and *glissando* strings; active; thinner than call 2; short pause.
1.55	4	Cloud of organlike string harmonies provides background for repeated high notes in xylophone; other *pizzicato* strings play unison repeated notes followed by *pizzicato* a second apart (like "chopsticks"); soft *pizzicato* strings play scale patterns in background; density remains constant for a long period; woodblock enters occasionally; sudden pause.
3.23	5	Overlapping *glissandi* and *pizzicato* strings fade out to end section.

Time	Call	
Time	*Call*	
0.00	1	Soft; veiled voice: ". . . the spiked wine letting cold silent . . ."; many sibilants, each followed by subtle ══════ and downward ***glissando***; echo effects and electronically superimposed vocal pedal-point patterns; ══════ and becomes more complex; then long silence.
1.00	2	New section; faint rapid electronic "chirping" sound in distance; accented outbursts of voiced sounds irregularly spaced with spurts of electronic twitterings and swishes; many sibilants.
1.50	3	Electronically produced ══════ to echo-chamber effects; ". . . so lonely . . ."; many changes in dynamics, texture, and complexity; much activity and ══════ with voice and electronic sounds, then gradually softer; section ends with irregular, quiet vocal sounds interspersed with silences; silence.
3.00	4	New section; chaotic bass of electronic sounds gradually transformed into sustained sounds resembling an organ; ══════ and increasing complexity followed by quieter section.
3.35	5	Sustained, bell-like sound, followed by fast-moving section with quick spurts of electronic sounds; overlapping vocal patterns treated in rapid echo; electronic twitterings.
4.00	6	Vocal sounds in medium range with occasional pitch and rhythm; heavy, complex electronic texture develops; then thinning, moving into higher register; long ══════ into silence.
5.00	7	Overlapping spurts of voice and electronic sounds; ". . . . soft word . . ."; followed by one long sustained note; sibilants and overlapping vocal patterns briefly continue.
5.35	8	Overlapping voice and electronic sounds continue; ". . . so sad . . ."; sibilants emphasized; occasional musical pitches and rhythms appear in vocal part; ══════ to fading end.

Measure	*Call*	
1	1	Percussive, vertical accents in several instruments at progressively shorter intervals: 7, 4, 2, and 1 seconds; short rhythmic motive dissolves into various rhythms in several instruments over roll of timpani; return to rhythmic motive over *glissando* of synthesized electronic sounds.
10	2	Hissing, scratching, and clicking sounds over low tone clusters in piano; violin *glissando* increases momentum; police whistle enters; short notes (*pizzicato*) and irregular spurts of electronic noise.
16	3	Louder; more complex texture; widely spaced clusters in piano alternating with short blasts on whistle; xylophone prominent; *pizzicato* in low strings; activity intensifies to climax; then immediate *glissando*, descending and ⟩ .
27	4	Violin plays *sul ponticello* (on the bridge) *tremolo* accompanied by timpani roll; electronic sound; hissing; resembles the idea of the first section (vertical accents); snare drum enters with rapid rhythmic patterns; ⟨ .
41	5	Loud as possible; all instruments playing at the same time; complex texture and rhythms; dissonant sounds; ends with a *glissando* that winds down in pitch and intensity.

Time	*Call*	
		Narrator discusses the music of John Cage.
0.00	1	Rhythmic music, sounds, and noises; blurred voice of announcer.
0.15	2	Sounds of Schubert Symphony 5, over which is quietly imposed the vigorous "Ritual Fire Dance" from *El Amor brujo* of Manuel de Falla; sounds of subway in background.
0.35	3	Woman's speaking voice (the message is clear); music continues sporadically.
0.50	4	Woman's narration continues: solo singing voice enters, later replaced by brief jazz-piano playing.
1.15	5	Woman's narration stops; orchestral march; sounds, noises, and background music; another woman's voice (". . . I spent $9.75 . . .") enters the web of sound; background music becomes more regular rhythmically; ⟶ along with unintelligible voices; man's laughter.

Time	*Call*	
0.00	1	Violins in extremely high register playing clusters of notes followed by high-register clusters in organ harmonium; very soft; static; successive entrances in lower strings playing harmonics; muted violins playing *sul ponticello* (on the bridge) fragments that end with upward *glissando*; vibraphone and flute play high-register clusters over horns, bassoons, and saxophone; winds build up from *pp* to *f* against cluster of static sound in lower strings; contrabassoon, tuba, percussion, organ, and piano enter briefly; string-cluster sound ⟹ .
1.35	2	Altos anticipate entrance of chorus; soft; static; successive entrances in other parts; thickening; becoming more dissonant; horns, trumpets, and trombone enter to complete dramatic ◁── .
2.02	3	Evangelist enters with spoken text ("Et surgens omnis multitudo. . .," "And the whole multitude of them . . .") against static cluster of sound in low register of alto voices; chorus enters in pitchless accent; trumpets and horns in trills increase thickness and dissonance; chorus enters with *glissando*; ──◁ to accent; timpani, woodblocks, lower strings, and low brass provide background for chorus speech sounds; ──◁ and *accelerando* to accent on "Christum regem esse" ("He is Christ the King").
2.35	4	Pitched bass solo ("Tu es rex Judaeorum," "Art thou the king of the Jews?"), followed by baritone solo ("Tu dicis," "Thou sayest"); chorus responds softly with "Domine"; jagged bass solo continues against static accompaniment of isolated pitches in trombones, contrabassoon, and horn.
3.10	5	Evangelist speaks ("Et remisit . . ." "And he sent . . ."); chorus enters with rapid nonpitched text against wide range of organ, string clusters, and isolated percussion sounds.
3.32	6	Tenors rapidly intone text; other parts enter on adjacent pitches creating a cluster of vocal sounds; bass solo ("Ecce nihil dignum morte actum" "He hath done nothing deserving of death") against cello and bass, then trombone and tuba in low register; spoken, loud entrance of chorus ending in "Barabbam" followed by spoken Evangelist ("Iterem autem Pilatus," "And Pilate again spoke to them"); percussion and strings ──◁ in background.
4.26	7	*Fortissimo* sung choral entrance on "Crucifige illum" ("Crucify Him"); bass solo ("Quid enim mali . . ." "Why, what evil . . .") against static accompaniment in double bass, then organ, then alone. Chorus again dramatically cries "Crucifige illum" in unison (and octaves) *ff*; horns, trumpets, trombones, tuba, percussion, organ, and lower strings play accented chords in a sharply dissonant *ff*.

Part 2   ∘   Perception charts

Measure	Call		
1	1	long notes above short notes	short notes above long notes
		lower part has no meter	lower part has definite meter feeling
		some accents	no accents
		upper part has no meter feeling	upper part has triple-meter feeling
20	2	long notes above short notes	short notes above long notes
		strong beat	weak beat
23	3	long notes above short notes	short notes above long notes
		lower part has no meter	lower part has definite meter feeling
		upper voice has some accents	upper voice has no accents
		lower voice is less active	lower voice is more active
29	4	long notes above short notes	short notes above long notes
		lower voice has no meter	lower voice has definite meter feeling
		upper voice has repeated patterns	upper voice has no patterns repeated

ANTONIO VIVALDI   Concerto for Violin and Orchestra in E, op. 8, no. 1, I (*La primavera*   Side 21, band 2
[*Spring*])

Measure	Call			
1	1	slow	moderately fast	very fast
		duple meter	triple meter	combination
		regular beat	irregular beat	
		accompaniment has complex pattern	accompaniment has simple pattern	
14	2	beat becomes weaker	beat remains strong	
		tempo changes	tempo remains same	
		several different patterns at same time	only one pattern present	
28	3	stronger beat	weaker beat	
		accompaniment has complex pattern	accompaniment has simple pattern	
31	4	duple meter	triple meter	combination
		regular beat	irregular beat	
		all long notes	all short notes	long and short notes
		rubato	no *rubato*	
		several different patterns in succession	patterns stay same	
37	5	all long notes	all short notes	long and short notes
41	6	strong beat	weak beat	
		repeated patterns present	no repeated patterns	
44	7	duple meter	triple meter	combination
		all long notes	all short notes	long and short notes
		beat becomes stronger	beat becomes weaker	
56	8	stronger beat	weaker beat	
		accompaniment has complex pattern	accompaniment has simple pattern	
59	9	heavy accents	no accents	
		all long notes	all short notes	long and short notes
66	10	stronger beat	weaker beat	
		mostly long notes	mostly short notes	
		all new patterns	patterns heard before	
76	11	duple meter	triple meter	combination
		irregular beat	regular beat	
		ends with *ritardando*	ends with *accelerando*	

Rhythm   114

WOLFGANG AMADEUS MOZART   Twelve Variations for Piano on "Ah, vous dirai-je,
Maman" in C, K. 265 (300*e*), variation XII

Measure	*Call*			
1	1	lower part more active	upper part more active	both parts equally active
		slow	fast	
		strong beat	weak beat	
		meter changes	meter remains the same	
9	2	lower part more active	upper part more active	both parts equally active
		rubato	no *rubato*	
		triple meter	duple meter	
		all long notes	all short notes	short and long notes
17	3	lower part more active	upper part more active	both parts equally active
		tempo changes	tempo remains same	
		weak beat	strong beat	
		new pattern	pattern heard before	
25	4	active pace	static pace	
		strong beat	weak beat	
		rubato	no *rubato*	

FRANZ PETER SCHUBERT *Die schöne Müllerin*, op. 25, no. 5: "Am Feierabend"
("At Leisure")

Measure	*Call*			
1	1	all long notes	all short notes	long and short notes
		fast	slow	
		strong beat	weak beat	
7	2	active	static	
		accents	no accents	
		fast	slow	
16	3	piano has mostly long notes	piano has mostly short notes	
		voice is *legato*	voice is *staccato*	
		irregular beat	regular beat	
26	4	strong beat	weak beat	
		piano has complex pattern	piano has simple pattern	
		accelerando at end	*ritardando* at end	
36	5	faster	slower	
		all strong accents	no accents	
		some *rubato*	no *rubato*	
		staccato	*legato*	both
45	6	piano has long notes	piano has short notes	
		fast	slow	
		staccato	*legato*	both
		strong beat	weak beat	
		some *rubato*	no *rubato*	
59	7	more active	more static	
		piano has mostly long notes	piano has mostly short notes	
		stronger beat	weaker beat	
		strong accents	weak accents	
		fast	slow	
		rubato	no *rubato*	
79	8	piano: fast, fast, slow	piano: slow, fast, slow	piano: slow only

Rhythm

Measure	Call			
1	1	duple meter	triple meter	
		staccato	*legato*	both
		active	static	
		regular beat	irregular beat	
		bass pattern keeps chang- ing	bass pattern keeps re- peating	
9	2	no *rubato*	some *rubato*	
		long notes	short notes	both
		several patterns repeated	no patterns repeated	
21	3	*staccato*	*legato*	both
		regular beat	irregular beat	
		more active	more static	
32	4	still more active	still more static	
		some *rubato*	no *rubato*	
		mostly long notes	mostly short notes	
		several patterns repeated	no patterns repeated	
46	5	beginning pattern is simple	beginning pattern is com- plex	
		tempo remains constant	tempo speeds and slows	
62	6	*staccato*	*legato*	both
		active	static	
		regular beat	irregular beat	
		duple meter	triple meter	
		bass pattern keeps chang- ing	bass pattern keeps re- peating	

Measure	Call			
1	1	slow	moderate	fast
		duple meter	triple meter	
		legato	*staccato*	both
		irregular beat	regular beat	
		no accents	some accents	
		patterns never repeated	patterns repeated	
33	2	slow	moderate	fast
		legato	*staccato*	both
		all long notes	all short notes	
		duple meter	triple meter	
51	3	weak beat	strong beat	
		new pattern	pattern heard before	
63	4	all *staccato*	all *legato*	
		no accents	some accents	
79	5	*staccato*	*legato*	
		patterns keep repeating	patterns not repeated	
107	6	no meter change	meter changes	
		changes to *legato*	changes to *staccato*	
		slow	moderate	fast
		duple meter	triple meter	

Rehearsal	Call			
129	1	very slow	moderate	very fast
		regular beat	irregular beat	
		melody has all short notes	melody has all long notes	melody has short and long notes
		accompaniment has simple pattern	accompaniment has complex pattern	
		accompaniment in mostly even notes	accompaniment in mostly uneven notes	
131	2	all short notes	all long notes	both
		repeated patterns present	no repeated patterns present	
132	3	added melody has all short notes	added melody has all long notes	added melody has short and long notes
		repeated patterns present	no repeated patterns present	
134	4	static	active	
		more complex rhythm	simpler rhythm	
		strong accents	weak accents	no accents
135	5	strong irregular accents	weak regular accents	
		mostly long patterns	mostly short patterns	
		all short notes	all long notes	both
138	6	static	active	
		strong regular accents	weak irregular accents	
		strong beat	weak beat	
139	7	very slow	moderate	very fast
		regular beat	irregular beat	
		melody has all short notes	melody has all long notes	melody has short and long notes
		accompaniment has simple pattern	accompaniment has complex pattern	
		accompaniment in mostly even notes	accompaniment in mostly uneven notes	

Measure	Call			
1	1	accents	no accents	
		mostly short notes	mostly long notes	
		triple meter	duple meter	
		simple, repeated patterns	complex, nonrepeated patterns	
10	2	mostly *staccato*	mostly *legato*	
		all short notes	some long notes	
18	3	some syncopation	no syncopation	
		mostly short notes	mostly long notes	
26	4	some syncopation	no syncopation	
36	5	strong accents	weak accents	no accents
		regular beat	no regular beat	
		mostly *staccato*	mostly *legato*	
52	6	strong accents	weak accents	no accents
		triple meter	duple meter	
		mostly short notes	mostly long notes	
68	7	solo is *staccato*	solo is *legato*	
		accompaniment has short notes	accompaniment has long notes	
98	8	regular beat	no regular beat	
		much *rubato*	no *rubato*	
		strong accents	weak accents	no accents
119	9	less active than call 8	more active than 8	
		staccato	*legato*	both
		beat very strong	beat weaker	
		syncopation in accompaniment	no syncopation in accompaniment	
149	10	many accents	no accents	
		some syncopation	no syncopation	
		staccato	*legato*	both
		repeated patterns	no repeated patterns	
177	11	alternation of *legato* and *staccato*	all *legato*	all *staccato*
		some accents	no accents	
189	12	regular beat	no regular beat	
		syncopation in every measure	only a few measures have syncopation	
		strong accents	weak accents	no accents

Measure	Call			
209	13	*staccato*	*legato*	both
		simple, repeated patterns	complex, nonrepeated patterns	
227	14	strong accents	weak accents	no accents
		accents become stronger at end	accents become weaker at end	
		ends *staccato*	ends *legato*	

Measure	Call		
None	1	simple rhythmic setting	complex rhythmic setting
		mostly steps	mostly leaps
		wide range	narrow range
	2	jagged melodic countour	smooth melodic contour
		strong rhythmic accents	no strong rhythmic accents
		narrow range	wide range
		one note per syllable	many notes per syllable (melismatic)
	3	remains syllabic	remains melismatic
		smooth melodic contour	jagged melodic contour
		range extended	range narrowed
		phrase becomes shorter	phrase becomes longer
		uses major scale	uses modal scale
	4	mostly stepwise	mostly leapwise
		smooth contour	jagged contour
	5	same melody and text as call 1	same melody and text as 3

Measure	Call			
1	1	trombone has steps	trombone has leaps	trombone has both
3	2	narrow range	wide range	
		downward	upward	
		voice with same melody as call 1	voice with different melody	
5	3	voice active	trombone active	
		voice in low register	voice in high register	
9	4	mostly small steps	mostly large leaps	
		several cadences	no cadences	
		voice in long, uninterrupted phrase	voice broken into short phrases	
		generally smooth contour	generally jagged contour	
18	5	mostly small steps	mostly large leaps	
		generally smooth	always jagged	
		no cadences	several cadences	
		voice more active	trombone more active	
34	6	generally smooth	generally jagged	
		generally upward	generally downward	
		mostly small steps	mostly large leaps	
40	7	leaps	steps	both
		becomes continuous	becomes interrupted	
		smooth	jagged	
		many cadences	no cadences	
51	8	chorus remains continuous	chorus remains interrupted	
		mostly small steps	mostly large leaps	
		long phrases	short phrases	
		several cadences	no cadences until end	

Measure	*Call*			
1	1	smooth contour	jagged contour	
		small steps	large leaps	both
		major	minor	other
		several short interrupted phrases	long uninterrupted phrase	
		generally low register	generally high register	
9	2	smooth contour	jagged contour	
		lower register than call 1	higher register than 1	
		several short interrupted phrases	long uninterrupted phrase	
		major	minor	
17	3	mostly small steps	mostly large leaps	
		mostly upward	mostly downward	
		several cadences	no cadences	
29	4	same melody as 1	same melody as 3	
		smooth contour	jagged contour	
		small steps	large leaps	both
		several short interrupted phrases	long uninterrupted phrase	
		generally low register	generally high register	
36	5	becomes major	becomes minor	
		several short interrupted phrases	long uninterrupted phrase	
		smooth becoming jagged	jagged becoming smooth	
45	6	becomes major	becomes minor	
		several short interrupted phrases	long uninterrupted phrase	both
		generally low register	generally high register	
51	7	smooth contour	jagged contour	
		small steps	large leaps	both
		several short interrupted phrases	long uninterrupted phrase	
		major	minor	
59	8	smooth contour	jagged contour	
		small steps	large leaps	both
		major	minor	
		several short interrupted phrases	long uninterrupted phrase	

Measure   *Call*

66   9

generally downward	generally upward	
several cadences	no cadences	
mostly large leaps	mostly small steps	
short notes	long notes	both
cadence in high register	cadence in low register	

FRANZ PETER SCHUBERT   *Die schöne Müllerin,* op. 25, no. 19: "Der Muller und der
Bach" ("The Miller and the Brook")

Measure	*Call*			
1	1	major	minor	other
		several cadences	no cadences	
		steps	leaps	both
29	2	major	minor	other
		steps	leaps	both
		no cadences	several cadences	
		mostly upward	mostly downward	upward and downward
61	3	major	minor	other
		short motives	long melodic line	
		same melody as call 1	same melody as 2	
		several cadences	no cadences	
		voice ends melody on tonic (key) tone	voice ends melody on other tone	

Measure	Call			
1	1	short interrupted phrases	long uninterrupted phrases	
		steps	leaps	both
		generally smooth contour	always jagged	
7	2	generally upward	generally downward	
9	3	three short phrases	one longer phrase	
12	4	steps	leaps	both
		all upward	all downward	upward and downward
18	5	generally smooth contour	generally jagged contour	
		generally upward	generally downward	
		melody embellished by orchestra	block chords only in orchestra	
29	6	narrow range	wide range	
		major	minor	
		long phrase line	short phrase line	
		primarily upward	primarily downward	

Measure	*Call*			
None	1	smooth contour	jagged contour	
		no cadences	some cadences	
		steps	leaps	both
	2	major	minor	other
		mostly small steps	mostly large leaps	
		several short interrupted phrases	long uninterrupted phrases	
	3	smooth contour	jagged contour	
		narrow range	wide range	
		generally higher register	generally lower register	
		moves to long high notes	moves to long low notes	
	4	steps	leaps	both
		phrases become shorter	phrases become longer	
	5	long notes	short notes	both
		wide range	narrow range	
		no cadences	some cadences	
	6	generally upward	generally downward	
		narrow range	wide range	
	7	steps	leaps	both
		some cadences	no cadences	
	8	moves to high register	moves to low register	
		steps	leaps	both
	9	melody uses repeated tones	melody uses no repeated tones	
		many steps	many leaps	

Measure	Call			
1	1	imitative polyphony	homophonic	nonimitative polyphony
		tonal	atonal	
		number of parts remains constant	number of parts varies	
16	2	imitative polyphony	homophonic	nonimitative polyphony
		number of parts remains constant	number of parts varies	
		cadence only at end	several overlapping cadences	
30	3	imitation begins one voice at a time	imitation begins between pairs of voices	
		imitation continues throughout section	no further imitation	
		number of parts remains constant	number of parts varies	
		strong cadence at end	no cadence at end	
42	4	melody with harmony	combination of homophonic and polyphonic	
		smooth harmonic contour	jagged harmonic contour	
		much dissonance	little dissonance	
58	5	imitative polyphony	homophonic	nonimitative polyphony
		number of parts remains constant	number of parts varies	

Measure	Call			
1	1	homophonic	polyphonic	
		combination of broken chords and block chords	all block chords	no chords
		major	minor	
1	2	homophonic	polyphonic	
		combination of broken chords and block chords	all block chords	no chords
		major	minor	
17	3	homophonic	polyphonic	mixed
		blending colors	contrasting colors	
		thin to thick	thick to thin	
		many cadences	no cadences	
44	4	homophonic	imitative polyphony	
		blending colors	contrasting colors	
		thin	thick	
		generally downward	generally upward	
52	5	homophonic	imitative polyphony	nonimitative polyphony
		thin	thick	
		block chords	no chords	
17	6	homophonic	polyphonic	mixed
		blending colors	contrasting colors	
		thin to thick	thick to thin	
		many cadences	no cadences	
44	7	homophonic	imitative polyphony	
		blending colors	contrasting colors	
		thin	thick	
		generally downward	generally upward	
52	8	homophonic	imitative polyphony	nonimitative polyphony
		thin	thick	
		block chords	no chords	
60	9	blending colors	contrasting colors	
		thin	thick	
		mostly short notes	mostly long notes	combination
68	10	homophonic	imitative polyphony	mixed
		begins thick, ends thin	begins thin, ends thick	
		begins major, ends minor	begins minor, ends major	
80	11	blending colors	contrasting colors	
		thin	thick	

Harmony and counterpoint

130

Measure	Call			
68	12	homophonic	imitative polyphony	mixed
		begins thick, ends thin	begins thin, ends thick	
		begins major, ends minor	begins minor, ends major	
80	13	blending colors	contrasting colors	
		thin	thick	
1	14	homophonic	polyphonic	
		combination of broken chords and block chords	all block chords	no chords
		major	minor	
17	15	homophonic	polyphonic	mixed
		blending colors	contrasting colors	
		thin to thick	thick to thin	
		many cadences	no cadences	
44	16	homophonic	imitative polyphony	
		blending colors	contrasting colors	
		thin	thick	
		generally downward	generally upward	
52	17	homophonic	imitative polyphony	nonimitative polyphony
		thin	thick	
		block chords	no chords	

Measure	Call			
1	1	homophonic	imitative polyphony	
		smooth harmonic shape	jagged harmonic shape	
		blending colors	contrasting colors	
		many cadences	no cadences	
10	2	violin melody with broken-chord accompaniment	imitative polyphony	hymnlike texture with violin embellishment
		blending colors	contrasting colors	
		thin accompaniment	thick accompaniment	
20	3	violin melody with broken-chord accompaniment	imitative polyphony	hymnlike texture with violin embellishment
		smooth harmonic shape	jagged harmonic shape	
		blending colors	contrasting colors	
31	4	imitative polyphony	hymnlike texture	
		thinner	thicker	
		many cadences	no cadences	
40	5	homophonic	polyphonic	
		block chords	no chords	
		frequent harmonic changes	infrequent harmonic changes	
45	6	homophonic	polyphonic	hymnlike
		block chords	broken chords	
		more frequent harmonic changes	less frequent harmonic changes	
		blending	contrasting	
56	7	homophonic	polyphonic	
		thick block chords	thin broken chords	
		accompaniment mostly short notes	accompaniment mostly long notes	
68	8	homophonic	polyphonic	
		accompaniment mostly short notes	accompaniment mostly long notes	
		accompaniment always present	accompaniment sometimes drops out	
79	9	homophonic	imitative polyphony	
		accompaniment mostly short notes	accompaniment mostly long notes	
		many chord changes	few chord changes	

Measure	Call			
83	10	homophonic	imitative polyphony	nonimitative polyphony
		thick	thin	
		block chords	broken chords	
		accompaniment active	accompaniment static	
86	11	hymnlike material with violin embellishment	violin melody with broken-chord accompaniment	
		thin	thick	
88	12	blending colors	contrasting colors	
		thinner	thicker	

FRANZ PETER SCHUBERT   *Die schöne Müllerin*, op. 25, no. 18: "Trock'ne Blumen"
("Withered Flowers")

Measure	Call			
1	1	tonal	atonal	
		homophonic	polyphonic	
		major	minor	other mode
		smooth harmonic contour	jagged harmonic contour	
		harmony is accompaniment	harmony is main content	
		few chord changes	no chord changes	
16	2	chords like call 1	new chords	
		major	minor	other mode
		several cadences	cadence at end only	
29	3	becomes more complex	becomes more simple	
		chords change slower	chords change faster	
		block chords only	block chords with melodic motive	
		moves to high register	moves to low register	
39	4	chords like 1	chords like 3	
		chords change slower	chords change faster	
		block chords only	block chords with melodic motive	
		thick becoming thin	thin becoming thick	
		moves to high register	moves to low register	
52	5	less complex chord changes	more complex chord changes	
		moves to low register	moves to high register	
		ends in major	ends in minor	ends in other mode

Harmony and counterpoint

Measure	Call			
1	1	homophonic	polyphonic	
		block chords	broken chords	no chords
4	2	homophonic	polyphonic	
		chords change slower	chords change faster	no chords
9	3	mostly low register	mostly high register	
		atonal	tonal	
12	4	homophonic	polyphonic	
		chords change like call 1	chords change like 2	
16	5	blending colors	contrasting colors	
		melody with static ac- companiment	melody with active ac- companiment	
20	6	broken chords	hymnlike	
		smooth harmonic shape	jagged harmonic shape	
24	7	melody with active ac- companiment	polyphony with chordal accompaniment	
		blending colors	contrasting colors	
		melody in low register	melody in high register	
		accompaniment in high register	accompaniment in low register	
39	8	blending colors	contrasting colors	
		thick	thin	
43	9	melody with active ac- companiment	block chords	
		thick getting thinner	thin getting thicker	
48	10	homophonic	polyphonic	
		getting thicker	getting thinner	

Measure	*Call*			
1	1	consonant	dissonant	
		thick	thin	
		jagged harmonic contour	smooth harmonic contour	
		simple harmonies	complex harmonies	
		combined block chords and broken chords	all block chords	
		clear cadences	unclear cadences	
10	2	tonal	atonal	
		polyphonic with harmonic material in piano	all block chords	
		all jagged	all smooth	combination
15	3	instruments in low register	instruments in high register	
		thick	thin	
		low accompaniment keeps changing texture	low accompaniment has constant texture	
18	4	homophonic	polyphonic	
		block chords	no chords	
		ends thinner	ends thicker	

Measure	*Call*			
1	1	generally thick	generally thin	
		loud	soft	
		primarily strings	primarily woodwinds	primarily brasses
65	2	thicker than call 1	thinner than 1	same density as 1
		oboe solo	flute solo	clarinet solo
		harpsichord and cello in bass	harpsichord and bassoon in bass	
		many accents	no accents	
		softer than 1	louder than 1	same dynamic level as 1
		much ⟨══⟩	no ⟨══⟩	
91	3	thinner than 2	thicker than 2	same density as 2
		softer than 2	louder than 2	same dynamic level as 2
		primarily strings	primarily woodwinds	primarily brasses
		keyboard instrument present	no keyboard instrument present	

Measure	Call			
1	1	accents	no accents	
		soft	loud	
		low register	high register	both
		flowing motion	interrupted motion	
4	2	thicker than call 1	thinner than 1	
		accents	no accents	
		soft	loud	
		strings prominent	woodwinds prominent	brasses prominent
		flowing motion	interrupted motion	
8	3	woodwinds become prominent	brasses become prominent	strings become prominent
11	4	melody line in violins	melody line in cellos	melody line in bassoons
13	5	accents	no accents	
		section ends with ——◁	section ends with ▷——	
16	6	some accents	no accents	
		only strings	only winds	both
		last chord thin and soft	last chord thick and loud	

Measure	*Call*			
1	1	all strings soft thick	woodwinds and strings loud thin	strings and brasses
9	2	all strings soft	woodwinds and strings loud	strings and trumpets
13	3	all strings thick	woodwinds and strings thin	strings and brasses
17	4	all strings soft	woodwinds and strings loud	strings and trumpets
21	5	violins and violas thick	violins and basses thin	cellos and basses
28	6	full orchestra thick	woodwinds and brasses only thin	
39	7	violins and violas	violins and basses	cellos and basses
47	8	full orchestra soft	woodwinds only loud	brasses only
55	9	strings thick	woodwinds thin	brasses

Measure	Call			
1	1	woodwinds and strings	brasses and strings	all strings
		much ——<—>——	no ——<—>——	
		soft	loud	
		density remains constant	density varies	
7	2	strings	woodwinds	brasses
		heavy accents	no accents	
14	3	alto and bass	soprano and alto	two altos
		accents	no accents	
		voice parts overlap	voice parts in hymnlike texture	
20	4	alto and bass	soprano and tenor	two tenors
		high register	low register	
26	5	getting thicker	getting thinner	
34	6	strings only	strings and woodwinds	brasses and strings
		thin	thick	
38	7	tenor	bass	
39	8	tenor	bass	
40	9	tenor and bass	soprano and alto	alto and tenor
41	10	tenor	bass	
42	11	tenor	bass	
43	12	tenor and bass	soprano and alto	alto and tenor

Tone color

Measure	*Call*			
1	1	main theme in cellos	main theme in violins	main theme in violas
		accompaniment in winds and *pizzicato* strings	accompaniment in winds and bowed strings	
		active accompaniment	static accompaniment	
		much ⤙⤚	no ⤙⤚	
12	2	theme in violas and flutes	theme in violins and oboes	
		accompaniment in winds	accompaniment in strings	
		active accompaniment	static accompaniment	
17	3	horn begins theme	trumpet begins theme	
		theme treated homo-phonically	theme treated poly-phonically	
		density of section is thin, thick, thin	density of section is thick, thin, thick	
27	4	strings prominent, winds accompany	winds prominent, strings accompany	
		generally downward and thinning	generally upward and thickening	
		section ends ⤚	section ends ⤙	
33	5	flute and oboe promi-nent	clarinet and bassoon prominent	
		oboe becomes prominent	clarinet becomes prom-inent	
		generally upper register	generally lower register	
		pizzicato-cello accom-paniment	bowed-cello accompani-ment	
37	6	woodwinds prominent	strings prominent	
		some ⤙⤚	no ⤙⤚	
		winds embellish	no winds	
40	7	woodwinds prominent	brasses prominent	
		brasses accompany	*pizzicato* strings accom-pany	
43	8	strings prominent	strings and winds promi-nent	
		thick	thin	
		generally upward	generally downward	
45	9	strings prominent	brasses prominent	
		winds added	no winds added	
		general ⤙	general ⤚	

Measure	Call			
53	10	strings and woodwinds prominent	brasses prominent	
		static and simple	active and complex	
		thick	thin	
		no accents	some accents	
57	11	strings and upper winds prominent	strings alone prominent	
		oboe has countermelody	bassoon has countermelody	
		no string *tremolo*	some string *tremolo*	
		no dynamic changes	some sudden dynamic changes	
60	12	woodwinds prominent	brasses prominent	
		accompaniment in *tremolo* strings	accompaniment in woodwind block chords	
62	13	theme in clarinet	theme in oboe	
		string countermelody	woodwind block chords	
64	14	fragments of theme played in contrasting colors	theme in cello	
67	15	bassoon prominent	oboe prominent	
		pizzicato-string accompaniment	bowed-string accompaniment	*pizzicato*- and bowed-string accompaniment
71	16	strings and woodwinds alternate	strings and brasses alternate	
		strings *pizzicato*	strings bowed	
73	17	violins have theme	cellos have theme	
		winds and strings accompany	only strings accompany	
		some ⟨ ⟩	no ⟨ ⟩	
80	18	flutes and horn have theme	violins and flutes have theme	
		no imitation used	short points of imitation follow	
		all blending colors	many contrasting colors	

Tone color

Measure	Call			
86	19	theme in strings	no theme, hymnlike texture	
		brasses and woodwinds have polyphony	brasses and woodwinds have block chords	
		thin	thick	
		static and simple	active and complex	
92	20	woodwinds and brasses prominent	woodwinds and strings prominent	
		thick	thin	
		much ——≺≻——	no ——≺≻——	
		ends ——≺	ends ≻——	
97	21	woodwinds prominent	brasses prominent	
		thinner	thicker	
99	22	strings prominent	woodwinds prominent	
		timpani accompany	cymbals accompany	
		flute added at end	clarinet added at end	oboe added at end
		general ——≺—— to end	general ≻—— to end	

Measure	*Call*			
1	1	piano starts	cello starts	string bass starts
		high register	low register	
4	2	voice speechlike (**Sprech-stimme**)	voice sings definite pitches	
		voice with French horn and trombone	voice with bass clarinet and cello	voice with violin and viola
		no ═══▷	some ◁══▷	
10	3	voice swoops from pitch to pitch	voice sings definite pitches	
11	4	*f* ═══▷ *pp*	*pp* ◁═══ *ff*	same dynamic level
		gets thicker	gets thinner	
		cello *pizzicato*	cello *tremolo*	
18	5	moves upward	moves downward	
		no ◁══▷	much ◁══▷	
23	6	**Sprechstimme**	voice sings definite pitches	
		generally upward	generally downward	
		moves into high register at end	moves into low register at end	
		ends with short accent	ends with long note	

Ambassador Satch

Time	*Call*			
0.00	1	introduction in piano alone	introduction in piano, string bass, and drums	
0.17	2	trumpet, clarinet, and trombone	trumpet, saxophone, tuba	clarinet, sax, and tuba
		accompaniment in drums, bass, piano	accompaniment in drums, piano	
		breaks between phrases in different instruments	breaks between phrases all in one instrument	
		two major breaks in trumpet	two major breaks: in trumpet, then clarinet	
1.22	3	introductory figure as in call 1	introductory figure now in entire band	
1.30	4	piano, bass, percussion	piano, percussion	bass, percussion
		break in piano, bass, percussion	break in piano alone	
2.01	5	bass solo with piano, percussion accompaniment	piano solo with bass, percussion accompaniment	percussion solo with bass, piano accompaniment
		solo has no ⇢ and ⇢	solo has some ⇢ and ⇢	
2.32	6	introductory figure as in 1	introductory figure in entire band	
2.40	7	sax solo	clarinet solo	trumpet solo
		accompaniment includes wind instrument	accompaniment includes no wind instrument	
		solo has no ⇢ and ⇢	solo has some ⇢ and ⇢	
3.12	8	trumpet solo	clarinet solo	trombone solo
		accompaniment includes wind instrument	accompaniment includes no wind instrument	
		solo has no ⇢ and ⇢	solo has some ⇢ and ⇢	
3.43	9	introductory figure again breaks in trombone smear	no introductory figure breaks in trumpet high notes	
		highest register in clarinet, then trumpet	highest register always in trumpet	
4.40	10	drum solo on one pitch level	drum solo on several pitch levels	
4.47	11	trumpet alone upward to cadence	trumpet and trombone upward to cadence	

Tone color   **145**

This form is: rondo   fugue   theme and   continuous   development sec-
                                                       variations   variations   tion of a sonata-
                                                                                            allegro

Measure	Call		
1	1	pattern *A*	
2	2	repetition of *A*	contrast
4	3	repetition of *A*	contrast
6	4	repetition of *A*	contrast
	1–4	Repeated	
8	5	repetition of *A*	pattern *B*
12	6	*A* varied	*B* varied
14	7	repetition of *A*	contrast
16	8	*A* varied	*B* varied
20	9	*A*	*B*
22	10	repetition of *A*	contrast
24	11	repetition of *A*	contrast
26	12	repetition of *A*	contrast
28	13	*B*	pattern *C*
32	14	*A* varied	*C* varied
36	15	*A* varied	*B* varied
38	16	repetition of *A*	contrast
40	17	*B*	*C*
44	18	*A*	contrast
46	19	repetition of *A*	contrast
48	20	repetition of *A*	contrast
50	21	repetition of *A*	contrast

This form is: sonata-allegro   minuet   fugue   rondo

Measure	*Call*			
Not given	1	*A* part of melody		
	2	*B* part of melody		
	3	*A* varied	*B* varied	new idea
	4	*A* varied	*B* varied	new idea
	5	*A* varied	*B* varied	new idea
	6	*A* varied	*B* varied	new idea
	7	*A* varied	*B* varied	new idea
	8	*A* varied	*B* varied	new idea
	9	*A* varied	*B* varied	new idea
	10	*A* varied	*B* varied	new idea
This form is:		fugue	rondo	theme and variations

Measure	*Call*			
1	1	main theme *A*		
28	2	repetition of *A*	new theme *B*	
56	3	Beginning of middle section, where themes are altered and reworked.		

This section is: exposition   development   recapitulation

Themes reworked
in this section
are: *A* only   *B* only   both *A* and *B*

| 76 | 4 | repetition of *A* | repetition of *B* | new melody *C* |
| 101 | 5 | repetition of *A* | repetition of *B* | repetition of *C* |

Section that brings back themes heard at first.

This section is: exposition   development   recapitulation

| 132 | 6 | Short conclusion, characterized by strong cadences. | | |

This section is: coda   ***ritornello***   overture

This form is: rondo   sonata-allegro   prelude   theme and variations

Measure	*Call*		
Section *A*			
Not given	1	Theme *A*	
	2	repetition of *A*	new theme *B*
	3	*A*	*B*
	4	material from *A*	material from *B*
	5	repetition of *A*	repetition of *B*
	6	material from *A*	material from *B*
Section *B*			
	7	repetition of *B*	new theme *C*
	8	repetition of *B*	repetition of *C*
	9	repetition of *C*	new theme *D*
	10	repetition of *C*	repetition of *D*
	11	repetition of *C*	repetition of *D*
	12	repetition of *C*	repetition of *D*
Section *A*			
	13	*A*	*B*
	14	*A*	*B*
	15	material from *A*	material from *B*

This form is: fugue   rondo   minuet and trio   theme and variations

This form is: continuous variations   theme and variations   free form   rondo   fugue

FRANZ PETER SCHUBERT   *Die schöne Müllerin*, op. 25, no. 5: "Am Feierabend"
("At Leisure")

Measure	*Call*					
1	1	introduction and section *A*				
26	2	*A* repeated	section *B*			
37	3	return to *A*	*B*	section *C*		
45	4	return to *A*	*B*	*C*	section *D*	
59	5	return to *A*	*B*	*C*	*D*	section *E*
76	6	coda				

Form

Measure	*Call*			
1	1	*A* melody		
9	2	*B* melody	repetition of *A* in higher register	
17	3	*A*	*B*	
29	4	*A*	*B*	*C* melody
37	5	*A*	*B*	*C*
45	6	varied repetition of *A*	varied repetition of *B*	varied repetition of *C*
51	7	*A*	*B*	*C*
59	8	repetition of *B*	repetition of *A* in higher register	
66	9	Ending section is:	stretto nocturne coda imitation	

Measure	*Call*			
1	1	*A* melody		
19	2	repetition of *A*	*B* section	
62	3	*A* melody	repetition of *B* section	
80	4	*A* section	*B* section	*C* section
121	5	*A* melody	repetition of *B* section	repetition of *C* section
135	6	*A* melody varied	*B* material	
172	7	*A* melody and extension	*B* material	*C* material
203	8	Ending section is: stretto	nocturne coda	imitation

Outline of this
  form is: *A B A C A B A*   *A A B B B A C*

This form is: rondo   theme and variations   concerto grosso   fugue

FRANZ PETER SCHUBERT   *Die schöne Müllerin*, op. 25, no. 7: "Ungeduld"
("Impatience)

Measure	Call				
Not given	1	introduction and section *A*			
	2	*A* repeated	section *B*		
	3	*A* repeated	*B*	section *C*	
	4	*A* repeated	*B*	*C*	section *D*
Outline of this form is:		*A A A A*	*A B B B*	*A B C D*	*A B A C*
This form is:		sonata-allegro	fugue	strophic	rondo

FRANZ PETER SCHUBERT *Die schöne Müllerin*, op. 25, no. 18: "Trock'ne Blumen"
("Withered Flowers")

Measure	*Call*				
1	1	introduction and section *A*			
16	2	*A* repeated	section *B*		
29	3	*A* repeated	*B*	*B* repeated	section *C*
39	4	*A* repeated	*B*	*B* repeated	*C*
52	5	piano material from *A*	piano material from *B*	piano material from *C*	

Measure	*Call*			
1	1	section *A*		
21	2	repetition of *A*	section *B*	section *A* varied
62	3	return of *A*	return of *B*	section *C*
Outline of this form is:		*A A A*	*A A B*	*A B A* *A B C*

Measure	*Call*			
None	None	small ensemble	large ensemble	
		all strings	all winds	strings and winds
		polyphonic	hymnlike	homophonic
		major	minor	other mode
		some imitation	no imitation	
		active	static	
		blending colors	contrasting colors	
		density remains generally the same	density changes frequently	
		no beat	weak beat	
		many obvious changes in dynamics	same general dynamic level throughout	
		no cadences	some cadences	
		no *rubato*	much *rubato*	
Style period:		classic	renaissance	modern

Measure	*Call*			
None	None	duple meter	triple meter	compound meter
		several cadences	no cadences	
		large ensemble	small ensemble	
		no imitation	some imitation	
		no continuo present	continuo present	
		polyphonic	mixed	homophonic
		major	minor	
		frequently repeated melody	continuous new melody	
		strong contrast between lower and upper parts	no contrast between lower and upper parts	
		shifting meters	same meter throughout	
		contrasting colors	blending colors	
Style period:		romantic	modern	baroque

ANTONIO VIVALDI   Concerto for Violin and Orchestra in E, op. 8, no. 1, II
(*La primavera* [*Spring*])

Measure	*Call*			
None	None	small ensemble	large ensemble	
		long, spun-out melody	short melody	
		narrow range	wide range	
		active pace	static pace	
		mostly major	mostly minor	
		repeated rhythmic pat-terns	no repeated rhythmic patterns	
		simple harmonic struc-ture	complex harmonic structure	
		no cadences	several cadences	
		homophonic	polyphonic	
		blending colors	contrasting colors	
		emphasis only on high parts	emphasis only on low parts	emphasis on both high and low parts
Style period:		baroque	romantic	classic

Measure	*Call*			
None	None	duple meter	triple meter	compound meter
		major	minor	
		much syncopation	no syncopation	
		two-note, half-step pattern in strings	three-note, leaping pattern in strings	
		continual string pattern	string pattern used only occasionally	
		same dynamic level throughout	uses louds and softs	
		some dissonance	all consonant	
		density of voices remains generally the same	density of voices changes frequently	
		weak final cadence	strong final cadence	
	Style period:	baroque	classic	romantic

Measure	*Call*			
1	1	major	minor	
		static	active	
		polyphonic	homophonic	
		theme in cello	theme in violin	theme in bassoon
8	2	main theme in oboe	main theme in clarinet	main theme in bassoon
		repeated patterns present in accompaniment	no repeated patterns present in accompaniment	
		no cadence at end	cadence at end	
16	3	return of main theme	new theme *B*	
		theme has jagged contour	theme has smooth contour	
		strings prominent	winds prominent	
		no ——◁▷——	much ——◁▷——	
30	4	return of main theme (varied)	return of theme *B*	
		theme in cello	theme in violin	
		some ——◁▷——	no ——◁▷——	
36	5	return of main theme	return of theme *B*	
		theme in winds	theme in strings	
		accompaniment in short notes	accompaniment in long notes	
		section ends with strings alone	section ends with winds alone	
51	6	return of main theme (varied)	return of theme *B*	
		accompaniment in strings only	accompaniment in winds only	accompaniment in winds and strings
56	7	*legato*	*staccato*	both
		jagged	smooth	
		moves upward	moves downward	both
60	8	hymnlike texture	imitative polyphony	
		some block chords	no block chords	
		no ——◁▷——	much ——◁▷——	
69	9	major	minor	
		main theme	theme *B*	new theme *C*
		accompaniment in broken chords	accompaniment in block chords	
		theme in woodwinds	theme in strings	theme in woodwinds and strings

Measure	Call			
76	10	thick block chords	broken chords	no chords
		no accents	accents	
80	11	hymnlike texture	nonimitative polyphony	
		melody in long notes and accompaniment in short notes	melody in short notes and accompaniment in long notes	
84	12	contrasting colors	blending colors	
		short notes	long notes	both
		repeated rhythm patterns	no repeated rhythm patterns	
		section ends with	section ends with	
		⸺⸺	⸺⸺	
96	13	melodic material in winds	melodic material in strings	
		accompaniment in broken chords	accompaniment in thick block chords	
		texture remains homophonic	thick block chords become main content	
101	14	generally upward	generally downward	
		only strings	winds and strings	
		harmony present	no harmony present	
105	15	major	minor	
		main theme	theme *B*	
		woodwinds and strings	strings alone	
114	16	homophonic	imitative polyphony	
		blending colors	contrasting colors	
		duple meter	triple meter	
		short notes	long notes	both
		density gets thicker	density gets thinner	
145	17	thick	thin	
		some accents	no accents	
		strings in low register	strings in high register	
150	18	hymnlike texture	polyphonic	
		all block chords	all broken chords	
		low register	high register	
154	19	main theme (varied)	theme *B* (varied)	
		major	minor	
		thin	thick	

Measure	Call			
158	20	static melody with active accompaniment	active melody with active accompaniment	
		strings only	brasses only	both
		strings move generally upward	strings move generally downward	
		strings are jagged	strings are smooth	
168	21	thinner	thicker	
		generally upward	generally downward	
173	22	main theme	theme *B*	
		theme in woodwinds	theme in strings	
		polyphonic	homophonic	
		accompaniment is static	accompaniment is active	
180	23	main theme	theme *B*	
		polyphonic	hymnlike	
		no block chords	some block chords	
		generally thick	generally thin	
		contrasting colors	blending colors	

FRÉDÉRIC FRANÇOIS CHOPIN   Polonaise in A♭, op. 53

Measure	Call			
1	1	thick introduction	thin introduction	
		long uninterrupted melody	short fragments	
		mostly *legato*	mostly *staccato*	
		upward	downward	both
		some ——◁▷——	no ——◁▷——	
17	2	melody *A*	introduction continues	
		no *rubato*	some *rubato*	
		simple melodic structure	complex melodic structure	
		melody is smooth	melody is jagged	melody is both
		some ——◁▷——	no ——◁▷——	
		long notes	short notes	both
		major	minor	other mode
33	3	new melody	same melody in higher register	
		no cadences	some cadences	
		generally thick	generally thin	
49	4	complex harmonic structure	simple harmonic structure	
		same register throughout	some changes in register	
		thick	thin	
		main melodic material	transition material	
57	5	return of melody *A*	new melody *B*	
		major	minor	other mode
		thinner than call 4	thicker than 4	
		regular beat	no beat	
		more active	less active	
61	6	repetition of melody *A* in higher register	repetition of melody *B* in higher register	
		generally upward	generally downward	
65	7	return of melody *A*	return of melody *B*	
		no *rubato*	some *rubato*	
		simple melodic structure	complex melodic structure	
		melody is smooth	melody is jagged	melody is both
		some ——◁▷——	no ——◁▷——	
		long notes	short notes	both

Style

Measure	Call			
81	8	new tonal center	same tonal center as 7	
		melody *A*	melody *B*	new melody *C*
		triple meter	duple meter	
		staccato	*legato*	both
		repeated patterns present	no repeated patterns present	
		loud	soft	both
96	9	new tonal center	same tonal center as 8	
		complex harmonic structure	simple harmonic structure	
		some accents	no accents	
105	10	short notes in treble against longer notes in bass	long notes in treble against shorter notes in bass	
		no *rubato*	some *rubato*	
		repeated patterns present	no repeated patterns present	
		generally soft	generally loud	
		section ends with ⟨⟩	section ends with ⟩	
114	11	melody *A*	melody *B*	melody *C*
		no *rubato*	some *rubato*	
		simple melodic structure	complex melodic structure	
		melody is smooth	melody is jagged	melody is both
		some ⟨⟩	no ⟨⟩	
		ends with thick block chords	ends with thin broken chords	
Style period:		modern	classic	romantic

Measure	*Call*			
None	None	tonal	atonal	
		active	static	
		several cadences	no cadences	
		major	minor	other mode
		large ensemble	small ensemble	
		polyphonic	hymnlike	
		chorus with accompani- ment	chorus with no accom- paniment	
		duple meter	triple meter	shifting meter
		density remains generally the same	density changes fre- quently	
		mostly jagged motion	mostly smooth motion	
		some ⟨═══⟩	no ⟨═══⟩	
		some dissonance	all consonant	
	Style period:	expressionistic	baroque	romantic

Measure	Call			
1	1	triple meter	duple meter	
		regular accents	irregular accents	
		thin	thick	both
		contrasting colors	blending colors	
23	2	mostly *staccato*	mostly *legato*	
		simple harmonic structure	complex harmonic structure	
		high sounds	low sounds	both
		irregular accents	no accents	
35	3	thick block chords	thin broken chords	
		weak accents	strong accents	
		repeated patterns present	no repeated patterns present	
60	4	imitative polyphony	nonimitative polyphony	
		contrasting colors	blending colors	
		loud chord at end	soft chord at end	
72	5	upward to irregular beat	downward to regular beat	
		contrasting colors	blending colors	
		generally thick	generally thin	
115	6	getting thinner	getting thicker	
		legato	*staccato*	both
		regular beat	irregular beat	
		one rhythmic pattern	several rhythmic patterns	
132	7	thinner than call 6	thicker than 6	
		accents	no accents	
		clarinet solo	piccolo solo	
149	8	triple meter	duple meter	
		thick	thin	
		simple harmonic structure	complex harmonic structure	
Style period:		romantic	modern	classic

Measure   *Call*

Song 1

None   1   generally smooth   generally jagged
               mostly large leaps   mostly small steps
               imitative polyphony   nonimitative polyphony
               traditional combination   unusual tone-color combi-
                 of tone colors   nation
               tonal   atonal
               beat is obvious   beat is not obvious

Song 2

         2   wide range   narrow range
               voice remains in same   voice has frequent regis-
                 register   ter changes
               polyphonic   homophonic
               instruments use tradi-   instruments use extreme
                 tional ranges   ranges

Song 3

         3   many short fragments   continuous melody
               duple meter   triple meter   no meter feeling
               wide range   narrow range
               remains in same register   frequent changes in regis-
                                            ter

Instrumental postlude

         4   smooth   jagged
               wide range   narrow range
               moves to strong cadence   moves to weak cadence
Style period: impressionistic   expressionistic   neoclassic

Measure	*Call*			
None	None	has a beat	has no beat	
		volume is constant	volume varies	
		texture changes smoothly	texture changes abruptly	
		some repetition of sounds	no sound is same twice	
		wide range of pitch	narrow range of pitch	
		steady pace	pace often changes	
		uses some definite pitches	uses no definite pitches	
		tonal	atonal	
		uses points of rest	uses no points of rest	
		uses traditional instru- ments	uses nontraditional sound source	
Style period:		classic	modern	romantic

Time	Call			
0.00	1	first sound has long and short notes	first sound has notes of same length	
		all upward	all downward	upward and downward
		electronic sound upward	electronic sound downward	
		no beat present	beat present	
0.16	2	bass pattern uses repeats	bass pattern uses no repeats	
		voice in narrow range	voice in wide range	
		tambourine sound on downbeats	tambourine sound on offbeats	
0.36	3	beat weaker	beat stronger	beat the same
		drum on downbeats	drum on offbeats	
		syncopation present	no syncopation	
		electronic sound upward	electronic sound downward	
1.04	4	new melody idea	melody repeated	
		electronic sounds on different pitches	electronic sounds on same pitch	
		general ⟍	general ⟋	
		drums get softer	drums get louder	drums stay the same
1.45	5	softer	louder	same dynamic level
		new melody idea	melody repeated	
		gets suddenly softer	gets suddenly louder	stays the same dynamic level
		electronic sounds upward only	electronic sounds downward only	electronic sounds upward and downward
		ends with overlapping directions	ends with one direction only